A Hopkins Commentary

A Hopkins Commentary

*An Explanatory Commentary
on the Main Poems, 1876–89*

Donald McChesney M.A.

*Senior Lecturer in English,
De la Salle College of Education, Middleton, Manchester*

New York · New York University Press
London · University of London Press Ltd

Library of Congress Catalog Card Number: 78-87080

Printed and bound in Great Britain by
Hazell Watson and Viney Ltd, Aylesbury, Bucks

Contents

Preface

*Since, as Solomon says, there is a time for everything
. . . it may be that the time will come for my verses.*
Hopkins

This book is a detailed analysis of Hopkins's main poems written between
1876 and 1889. It is intended for the average student who wishes to come
to a better understanding of the poet. The more advanced student, though
able to dispense with much of the explanatory material, will, I hope, find
guidelines for further study in the background material supplied.

Everywhere possible, Hopkins's letters and notebooks have been used
and quoted to elucidate the poems. They cast fascinating light on Hopkins
the man; they show also the association-patterns, the personal stresses and
strains, the attitudes to experience and the intense preoccupation with the
sound-values of language that went into producing the poems. Source
references are given in all places.

There are separate explanatory sections on 'Inscape', 'Instress' and on
the ideas of Duns Scotus, to fill out the philosophical and psychological
background to Hopkins's poetry. There is also a fairly full section on his
poetic techniques, such as the use of sprung rhythm, *cynghanedd* and the
'lettering' of syllables to which he devoted such care.

Late in his life, Hopkins wrote to Bridges of his resolution 'to fix short
prose arguments' to some of his pieces. Epic poetry, drama, and ballad,
he continued, should be immediately intelligible, 'but everything need not
and cannot be':
*Plainly if it is possible to express a subtle and recondite thought on a subtle
and recondite subject in a subtle and recondite way and with great felicity
and perfection, in the end, something must be sacrificed.*
(*B*, 265)

What is sacrificed in this search for profundity, style and terseness is
intelligibility—'the being at once, nay perhaps even the being without
explanation at all, intelligible' (*B*, 266).

In cases of obscurity therefore I have offered some 'prose arguments'.
They are not paraphrases, but simply maps of the syntactical structure of
specially involved passages. No logical prose statement can, however,

render what Hopkins 'meant' in any given passage, because it inevitably leaves out the rich content conveyed through line-rhythm, the complex patterning of vowel and consonant, and the multiple association which make a poem, especially a Hopkins poem, incommunicable in any terms other than itself.

Otherwise the inclusion of prose statements to elucidate difficult passages needs no further justification. If the reader can be delivered from the search for the merely logical sense of some of Hopkins's utterances, he will have more time to appreciate the peculiar intensity of his modes of expression and the new voice he found for poetry. Even his obscurity has its prevailing characteristics which, once grasped, will enable the reader to progress unencumbered by notes.

Many topics not separately treated in the explanatory sections will be found discussed as they arise in individual poems, and the reader is urged to consult the index for all reference to any given topic.

If at any point I have been guilty of over-explanation or of labouring the obvious, it is because I have had in mind the needs of those students whose culture and language is not British nor even European. Hopkins is difficult enough at times, even for English-speaking people who share some of his cultural and linguistic background, and the full scope of the problems he must present to the non-European student is difficult to envisage. However, some attempt has been made, and I am encouraged by some words of Hopkins, written a year before he died:

. . . we should explain things, plainly state them, clear them up, explain them; explanation—except personal—is always pure good; without explanation people go on misunderstanding; being once explained they henceforward understand things; therefore always explain.

(*B*, 275)

D. McC.

To John Killeen

Acknowledgments

I am most grateful to the staff of Rochdale Public Libraries for their consistent help in obtaining books for me and for their constant endeavour to meet even my most unreasonable requests for extended loan-periods.

I would also like to thank all those who have read various sections of this book and assisted me with comment and advice. My appreciation is also due to Mr Andrew Wilton of the Walker Art Gallery, Liverpool, who went to much trouble for me on a small but important matter.

D. McC.

The author and publishers are indebted to Oxford University Press for permission to include the sonnet with which Robert Bridges prefixed the first edition of Hopkins's *Collected Poems*, and to quote copyright material from a number of works (listed in full on p. xi).

Abbreviations Used

AV   Authorized Version of the Bible.

B   *The Letters of Gerard Manley Hopkins to Robert Bridges*, edited by Claude Colleer Abbott. Oxford University Press (London, revised ed., 1955).

D   *Correspondence of Gerard Manley Hopkins and R. W. Dixon*, edited by Claude Colleer Abbott. Oxford University Press (London, revised ed., 1956).

FL   *Further Letters of Gerard Manley Hopkins* (Including his Correspondence with Coventry Patmore), edited by Claude Colleer Abbott. Oxford University Press (London, 2nd ed., 1956).

J   *The Journals and Papers of Gerard Manley Hopkins*, edited by Humphry House and Graham Storey. Oxford University Press (London, 1959).

L   G. F. LAHEY, S.J., *Gerard Manley Hopkins*. Oxford University Press (London, 1930).

N   *Note-books and Papers of Gerard Manley Hopkins*, edited by Humphry House. Oxford University Press (London, 1937). (Reissued as 2 vols., 1959.)

RSV   Revised Standard Version of the Bible.

S   *The Sermons and Devotional Writings of Gerard Manley Hopkins*, edited by C. Devlin, S.J. Oxford University Press (London, 1959).

WHG   W. H. GARDNER, *Gerard Manley Hopkins; A Study of Poetic Idiosyncrasy in Relation to Poetic Tradition*, 2 vols. Secker & Warburg (London, 1943); 2nd ed. Oxford University Press (London, 1962).

Introduction

Gerard Manley Hopkins 1844-89

Early childhood

Gerard Manley Hopkins was born at Stratford, Essex, on 28 July 1844, the eldest of a family of eight. His father, Manley Hopkins, Consul General of the Hawaiian Islands to Great Britain, was a man of many parts who wrote works as diverse as a History of Hawaii, a book on marine insurance and a volume of poems, *Spicilegium Poeticum*.

Gerard's mother, daughter of Samuel Smith, a fashionable London physician, was a woman of gentle nature, highly educated and acquainted with German literature and metaphysics. From her, Gerard inherited a philosophical bent and a decided talent for artistic draughtsmanship. His poetic gifts were most likely from the paternal side.

Hopkins's early precocity in the arts was fostered by an aunt who lived with the family during his childhood. She herself was a musician and portrait painter, and she found a ready pupil in Gerard, whose strong talents in these directions can be seen from his extant drawings,[1] as well as from the music and lyrics which he loved to compose and sing at musical entertainments during his life in the Society of Jesus.

School

In 1852 the family moved from Stratford to Oak Hill, Hampstead. Hopkins first attended day school there, then moved in 1854 to Sir Robert Cholmondley's Grammar School at Highgate, a school already distinguished by such names as Coleridge, Lamb, and De Quincey. Here Hopkins met Ernest Hartley Coleridge, grandson of the poet, and also Marcus Clarke, later to rise to fame in Australian letters. The latter was described by Hopkins as a 'kaleidoscopic, parti-coloured, harlequinesque, thaumotropic being', which is no great guide to the appearance of Clarke, but reflects a startling vocabulary in the then twelve-year-old author. Clarke, later in life, featured Hopkins in a story as 'Gerard, my boy-friend, who fled from Oxford to Stonyhurst and embraced the discipline of Loyola'.[2]

At school, Hopkins showed that characteristic mixture of physical frailty and almost forbidding moral courage that marked—in more than one sense—his whole life. On one occasion, just to prove a point, he abstained from all liquid till he collapsed, and on another occasion

---

[1] *Handsomely reproduced in J.*
[2] *Recorded by Father Lahey; L, 5*

abstained from salt for a week. He did not take much part in games, and his lifelong friend Canon Dixon, then a tutor at the school, remembered him as 'a pale young boy, very light and active, with a very meditative and intellectual face' (*D*, 4). Although no athlete, Hopkins was strong for his size and was apparently given to climbing to giddy heights on trees.

Even in these early days he wrote poetry and won two school prizes for it. One was a heavily decorated Miltonic-Keatsian piece called 'The Escorial':

He rang'd long corridors and cornic'd halls,
And damasqu'd arms and foliag'd carving piled—
With painting gleamed the rich pilastered walls—
Here play'd the virgin mother with her Child
In some broad palmy mead and saintly smiled,
And held a cross of flowers in purple bloom;
He, where the crownals droop'd, himself reviled
And bleeding saw . . .

The other poem, which won the prize in 1862 was a piece of unrestrained sensuous luxury, outrivalling the early Keats, called 'The Vision of the Mermaids':

. . . the west had grown
To an orb'd rose, which, by hot pantings blown
Apart, betwixt ten thousand petalled lips
By interchange gasped splendour and eclipse.
The zenith melted to a rose of air;
The waves were rosy-lipp'd; the crimson glare
Shower'd the cliffs and every fret and spire
With garnet leaves and blooms of rosy-budded fire.

This soft, loose material is a strange beginning for a poet whose later utterance was to go to the limits of tension and austerity.

Oxford, 1863–7

In 1863, having won a scholarship, Hopkins proceeded to Balliol College, Oxford, where the course of his life was to be changed. The university was, at the time, in a state of religious ferment, with German metaphysics, and accompanying liberal-rationalism, making great inroads upon the student mind, against a stout resistance being offered by the fervent and brilliant men of the Anglican Oxford Movement. Newman, one of its great founder-members, had gone over to the Roman Catholic faith, but men like Pusey and Liddon, staunch adherents of the Anglican middle way, were still unearthing ancient Christian wealth of dogma and liturgy in an attempt to stem the tide. Hopkins was naturally drawn to this movement, as much by its aesthetic as by its religious appeal. He was attracted also to Walter Pater, who stood outside these main camps, but who taught a religion of beauty, drawing a large following of students by his advocacy of the search for the 'intense moment' of experience and for the life which 'burns with a hard and gem-like flame'.

It is not surprising therefore to find Hopkins beginning to enter upon Lenten ascetic practices. An 1865 poem entitled 'Easter Communion' begins:

Pure fasted faces draw unto this feast:
God comes all sweetness to your Lenten lips.
You striped in secret with breathtaking whips . . .

The above lines are not necessarily a guide to Hopkins's actual practice at the time, but many of his Anglo-Catholic acquaintances were practising penitential exercises, and his impulses were turning this way. A resolution from his diary of January 1866 records:

For Lent. No pudding on Sundays. No tea except if to keep me awake and then without sugar. Meat only once a day. No verses in Passion Week or on Fridays. No lunch or meat on Fridays. Not to sit in armchair except can work in no other way. Ash Wednesday and Good Friday bread and water. (*J*, 72)

Hopkins and Robert Bridges

At Oxford, Hopkins met Robert Bridges, and began one of the most enduring friendships of his life. The friendship was to be conducted chiefly by correspondence, without which we would know very little of Hopkins's private thoughts and feelings during his comparatively short working life. As it is, in a volume of correspondence which will itself one day become a classic, we have his opinions on a great variety of matters from politics to poetics, and a richly documented record of his life from his early Jesuit training right to the year of his death.

Bridges was born in 1844, the same year as Hopkins, but lived till 1930, forty-one years longer than his friend. He went to Eton, then to Corpus Christi College, Oxford. He subsequently studied medicine at St Bartholomew's Hospital, practised it for a time, then retired, to spend the rest of his life in semi-seclusion, studying and writing. His first volume of poetry, which he later tried to suppress, was published in 1873, and the years to 1894 saw more volumes of lyrics plus such works as *Prometheus the Firegiver* and *Eros and Psyche*. He became Poet Laureate in 1913 and received some acclaim for his anthology *The Spirit of Man*. He died in 1930, full of years and full of honours.

Bridges's poetic work is somewhat scholarly and frigid, though of a high standard of learned craftsmanship, as befits the author of an extremely detailed work on Milton's prosody. It may be that future generations will value him more for himself, but at present the greatest debt we owe him is the preservation of the memory of Hopkins, and the slow introduction, to an unaccepting world, of the latter's poems. For years he was content to insert a few scattered pieces by Hopkins into anthologies, and not till 1918 did he launch a first edition, lovingly prepared and edited. Even so, it took many years to exhaust the first printing of 2,000 copies, and it was not till the 1930s that Hopkins's reputation began to grow. As he completed the book in January 1918, while the Great War was ravaging Europe, Bridges mourned and loved his long-dead friend in a moving sonnet with which he prefaced the book:

Our generation already is overpast,
And thy lov'd legacy, Gerard, hath lain
Coy in my home; as once thy heart was fain
Of shelter, when God's terror held thee fast
In life's wild wood at Beauty and Sorrow aghast;
Thy sainted sense trammel'd in ghostly pain,
Thy rare ill-broker'd talent in disdain:
Yet love of Christ will win man's love at last.
Hell wars without; but, dear, the while my hands
Gathered thy book, I heard, this wintry day,
Thy spirit thank me, in his young delight
Stepping again upon the yellow sands.
Go forth: amid our chaffinch flock display
Thy plumage of far wonder and heavenward flight!

Hopkins once wrote to Bridges that he was quite content to leave the fate of his poems to the hands of Providence, and who would deny, in his unusual circumstances, that he was right?

Conversion to the Roman Catholic faith—Oxford, 1866

On 21 October 1866 Hopkins was received into the Roman Catholic Church by Father (later Cardinal) Newman. It was not an isolated conversion, as many young men at Oxford, including his close friend William Addis, had preceded him, and many more were to follow. 'All our minds you see were ready to go at a touch,' he wrote to Newman, 'and it cannot but be that the same is the case with many here' (*FL*, 30). The Tractarian Movement (later called the Oxford Movement), had done its work only too well. Searching into the well-springs of revelation and dogma to do battle against rationalism, many of its Anglican adherents, following the great Newman, had found themselves impelled towards Rome.

It was bitter for such men as Pusey and Liddon, devoted supporters of Anglicanism, to see this Romeward flow of talent, brains and fervour. Canon Liddon, Hopkins's onetime confessor, wrote four urgent appeals to Hopkins imploring him to think twice about the historical validity of Papal claims, suggesting that friendship with Addis was the real cause of his proposed move, urging him to rethink the whole business before making 'a very serious mistake indeed', demanding that he should examine 'the English case', and casting doubt on the wisdom of Hopkins's choice of Newman as mentor.

It was all to no avail. Hopkins wrote later that if anyone ever became a Catholic 'because two and two make four', he did. He meant that he was intellectually convinced of the logical validity of Catholic arguments and would have gone over to Rome whatever the inward or outward obstacles. Also, there was, in his nature, a deep-seated hunger for absolute obedience to strong authority, which could be met only in the Roman Church of the time. This hunger was the obverse side of the streak of wilfulness which lay half-hidden in him; it was also his defence against the uncertainty and waywardness of his emotional nature which he described in 'The Wreck of the Deutschland' as 'soft sift in an hourglass'.[3]

His letters at the time reveal a characteristic blend of integrity and stubborn legalistic obstinacy. This, for instance, to his father:

My dear Father,

I must begin with a practical immediate point. The Church strictly forbids all communion in sacred things with non-Catholics. I have only just learnt this, but it prevents me going to chapel, and so yesterday I had to inform the Dean of Chapel. Today the Master sent for me and said he cd. not grant me leave of absence without an application from you. As the College last term passed a resolution admitting Catholics and took a Catholic into residence it has no right to alter its principle in my case. I wish you therefore not to give yourself the pain of making this application, even if you were willing . . .

(*FL*, 91)

Considering that at the time of writing he was not yet received into the Catholic Church there is as much of wilfulness as of obedience in this stubborn adoption of a bounden duty that was not yet strictly his, even though it was soon to become his. This is the young Hopkins, recalled in after years by a school acquaintance, C. N. Luxmoore, a Hopkins who 'only bristled the more, when as was usually the case the authorities tried force and browbeating' (*FL*, 395).

The only pangs suffered by Hopkins at the time of his conversion were

[3] '*The Wreck of the Deutschland*', st. 4.

those caused by the distress of his loyally Anglican parents. His father wrote to Liddon:

He writes in an impassioned style about 'adoring the five blessed wounds' & c, & speaks with perfect coldness of any possible estrangement from us, who have loved him with an unchanging love. His mother's heart is almost broken by this, & by his desertion from our Church, her belief in, & devotion to, which are woven in with her very being.
(*FL*, Appendix IV, p. 435)

Hopkins wrote to Newman that he could not bear to look twice at his parents' letters.[4] After his reception however reconciliation was not long in coming, and all was well.

The finding of his vocation

In the spring of 1867 Hopkins graduated with a Double First in Greats. It was not for nothing that the august Benjamin Jowett had called him the star of Balliol. After a vacation on the continent he returned, at Newman's suggestion, to the Oratory School at Birmingham, as a teacher. He was not particularly happy here, and in a letter to a friend Baillie there is the first mention of that nervous weakness that was to plague him for the rest of his life:

I must say that I am very anxious to get away from this place. I have become very weak in health and do not seem to recover myself here or likely to do so. Teaching is very burdensome, especially when you have so much of it: I have. I have not much time and almost no energy—for I am always tired— to do anything on my own account.
(12 February 1868; *FL*, 231)

He was not to be here long, however, for he had at last found what in an earlier poem he had called,

      ... the dominant of my range and state—
Love, O my God, to call Thee Love and Love.
(Sonnet: 'Let me be to Thee as the circling bird')

In his case it was to be a life spent serving God under the severe discipline of the Society of Jesus. 'I do not think there is another prospect so bright in the world', he wrote to his mother (*FL*, 49).

I am both surprised and glad at your news [wrote Newman] *.... I think it is the very thing for you ... Don't call 'the Jesuit discipline hard', it will bring you to heaven. The Benedictines would not have suited you.*
(*FL*, Appendix III, p. 408)

It is perhaps useless to speculate, as many have done, about the human wisdom or folly of the decision, and about whether Hopkins the poet was crushed

[4] *FL, 29.*

by the hardness of Jesuit life. Luxmoore, reminiscing long afterwards, wrote that 'humanly speaking he made a grievous mistake', but concluded, 'Any wood will do for the cross, when God's perfection is thereby reached' (*FL*, Appendix I, p. 396). The choice Hopkins made was the outward sign of his secret and personal destiny. The sufferings which were to come—which stemmed from his frail yet arduous nature, rather than from his choice of life—were part of the process of his sanctification, and accepted as such; and his poetry was struck like fire from the tensions in his life.

Jesuit training, 1868–77

In September 1868 Hopkins went to the Jesuit Noviciate at Manresa House, Roehampton. He had already burned his early poems, a deliberate and painful act of oblation that was to set the tone for the rest of his life. A Journal entry of 11 May of that year reads, simply, 'Slaughter of the innocents' (*J*, 165). He explained himself later to the gentle Dixon, who must have been horrified at such drastic action. It was a question of putting first things first:

This I say: my vocation puts before me a standard so high that a higher can be found nowhere else. The question then for me is not whether I am willing . . . to make a sacrifice of hopes of fame . . . but whether I am not to undergo a severe judgment from God for the lothness I have shown in making it . . . for the backward glances I have given with my hand upon the plough.
(*D*, 88)

In his poem on the martyr, Margaret Clitheroe, Hopkins wrote of 'God's counsel columnar-severe', and the severity is certainly displayed here, though luckily most of the poems survive.

He was to write no more till 1875, when 'The Wreck of the Deutschland' was written at the prompting of his superior. Although he continued to write poems from then on, he was always scrupulously careful to avoid even legitimate chances of publication. As Father Devlin points out, his horror of public esteem was exaggerated:

His poetic genius was his very essence, his 'inscape', his special likeness to the Divine Essence. Yet Hopkins the Jesuit behaved to Hopkins the Poet as a Victorian husband might to a wife of whom he had cause to be ashamed. His muse was a highborn lady, a chaste matron, dedicate to God; but he treated her in public as a slut, and her children as an unwanted and vaguely sinful burden.

(Introduction to Hopkins's Spiritual Writings; *S*, 119)

It was a rejection which proceeded not from the rigour of the Jesuit Order, but from his own stubborn hardness towards himself.

After a year at Manresa, Hopkins proceeded to Stonyhurst College, near

Whalley, Lancashire, where he spent three years in the study of philosophy, followed by a year back at Roehampton teaching rhetoric, including a course on poetry and verse. Then in August 1874 he was sent to St Beuno's College, near St Asaph, Flintshire, North Wales, where he spent three happy and fruitful years completing his studies and his spiritual formation. He described the place to his father:

The house stands on a steep hillside, it commands the long-drawn valley of the Clwyd to the sea, a vast prospect, and opposite is Snowdon and its range, just now it being bright visible but coming and going with the weather. The air seems to me to be very fresh and wholesome.

(29 August 1874; *FL*, 124)

Even in these ideal conditions, however, the weakness and melancholy which were to make his later years an inward crucifixion were present from time to time. But he was more free from his affliction here than he was ever to be again, saving only his year of tertianship in 1881–2.

Three years of rural peace, religious discipline and contemplation completed his transformation as man and poet. After the years of silence the poetic fire that broke from him then was, to use his own metaphor,[5] a billion times told lovelier—in the sense of being charged with energy and tension—than anything he had previously written. His was a new-made vision, born of discipline and ascesis, of a Creation bursting with the energy and beauty of God.[6] It was expressed in a new and strange idiom, highly wrought and idiosyncratic, employing a new and sophisticated range of rhetorical techniques.[7]

Jesuit Priest: 1877–89 (death)

On 23 September 1877 Hopkins was ordained priest. It was his year of grace in other ways also, because he produced ten poems. The next four years were to be spent in a variety of posts in various places, the first being at Mount St Mary's College, Chesterfield (October 1877–May 1878), where he acted as bursar and sub-minister. He was none too happy here, and wrote to Bridges:

Write me an interesting letter. I cannot do so. Life here is as dank as ditch-water and has some of the other qualities of ditchwater: at least I know that I am reduced to great weakness by diarrhoea, which lasts too, as if I were poisoned.

(*B*, 47)

[5] See 'The Windhover'.
[6] See 'God's Grandeur' and 'Hurrahing in Harvest'.
[7] See section Hopkins and the Art of Rhetoric, p. 14, and following section on Sprung Rhythm, p. 16.

His muse 'turned utterly sullen' here, and he wrote nothing except 'The Loss of the Eurydice'.

He proceeded from Chesterfield to Stonyhurst, where he spent two months (May–June 1878) and wrote 'The May Magnificat'. He was then sent for the rest of the year to the fashionable Jesuit Church at Farm Street, London. It was here that he regaled a sophisticated metropolitan congregation with the comparison of the Church to a cow with full udders, wandering the world, willing to part with the milk of salvation to whomsoever cares to milk her.

His next stop (December 1878–October 1879) was at St Aloysius's, Oxford, where he was curate and also Chaplain to Cowley Barracks. Although he was never very settled here, not getting on too well with his superior, Father Parkinson, and not being greatly enamoured of his somewhat critical flock, he wrote a number of poems including 'The Bugler's First Communion'. He was therefore relieved to be moved to St Joseph's, Bedford Leigh, Lancashire, his first industrial parish.

He spent only three months here, but he was happy. In this grimy and squalid little place in the wastes of East Lancashire—he described in one letter the clouds of sulphuretted hydrogen gas rolling on the pavements of nearby St Helens—he found a people that needed him and responded to him. He even lapsed into the occasional homely Lancashire idiom, in sermon and poem.[8] Father Devlin writes that it was an idyllic interlude in his priestly life.[9] It was his next move to Liverpool (30 December 1879) that was to blight his spirit and fill him with weariness and disgust at the mass degradation caused by Victorian industrialism.

His appointment was to the large Jesuit Church of St Francis Xavier, Salisbury Street, a heavily populated area of Liverpool. His letters to Bridges and Dixon during the two years he spent here are often light, learned and amusing, until he touches upon his personal feelings, when the underlying affliction becomes apparent:

I take up a languid pen to write to you, being down with diarrhoea and vomiting, brought on by yesterday's heat, and the long hours in the confessional. Yesterday was in Liverpool the hottest day in the year.

(*B*, 104)

I remarked for the thousandth time with sorrow and loathing the base and bespotted figures and features of the Liverpool crowd. When I see the fine and manly Norwegians that flock hither to embark for America walk our streets and look about them it fills me with shame and wretchedness.

(*B*, 127)

[8] *See note on 'all road ever' (line 8) in poem 'Felix Randal', p. 111.*
[9] *S. 5.*

These passages are symbolic of the malaise that beset him in Liverpool. A more robust spirit and constitution would have viewed things differently, but for him it was fatigue, lassitude, depression and disgust. He worked on willingly, but confessed himself 'so fagged, so harried and gallied up and down' with endless labours. His poetic vein dried up, in what he described as that 'museless place'. He accepted it as best he could, but his frailty of constitution began to tell on him, and his willing spirit began to flag.

In August 1881 his Liverpool stay came to an end and he received a much-needed break in the form of an eleven-month period of Tertianship at Manresa House, Roehampton. Tertianship, he wrote to Dixon, is a preparation for final vows:

It is in preparation for these last vows that we make the tertianship; which is called a schola affectus *and is meant to enable us to recover that fervour which may have cooled through application to study and contact with the world.*

(*D*, 75)

The amiable Dixon could never quite accept that Hopkins could really want to be a Jesuit, so we find the latter confirming the wholeheartedness of his vows:

I make them to myself each day, so that I should be black with perjury if I drew back now. And beyond that I can say with St Peter: To whom shall I go? Tu verba vitae aeternae habes.[10]

(ibid.)

He wrote also of the complete happiness of the secluded contemplative life which, as a working Jesuit, he knew was not to be his:

. . . my mind is here more at peace than it has ever been and I would gladly live all my life, if it were so to be, in as great or a greater seclusion from the world and be busied only with God.

(ibid.)

The last seven years

He emerged refreshed from the Tertianship in September 1882, and was sent to teach classics at Stonyhurst. It was at this time that he met Coventry Patmore, who, though to the end unable to understand Hopkins's poetry— 'veins of pure gold embedded in impracticable quartz'—instantly recognized the rare quality of Hopkins the man. 'I have seldom felt so much attracted towards any man as I have been towards him', he wrote to Bridges, and so greatly was he moved by the integrity of mind of the younger man that he was actually moved to burn the MS of 'Sponsa Dei' at

[10] *'Thou hast the words of eternal life', Peter's words to Christ (John, vi, 68).*

a chance disapproving remark made by the latter. After Hopkins's death, Patmore wrote to Bridges:

I can well understand how terrible a loss you have suffered in the death of Gerard Hopkins—you who saw so much more of him than I did. I spent three days with him at Stonyhurst, and he stayed a week with me here; and that, with the exception of a somewhat abundant correspondence by letter, is all the communication I had with him; but this was enough to waken in me a reverence and affection, the like of which I have never felt for any man but one.

(Quoted by Father Lahey, *L*, 52–3)

Patmore went on to speak of the saintly quality of Hopkins, and concluded:

. . . there was something in all his words and manners which were at once a rebuke and an attraction to all who could only aspire to be like him.

(ibid.)

At the beginning of 1884, Hopkins was elected to a fellowship in Classics at the Royal University of Ireland. Since the latter was, at the time, purely an examining body, Hopkins was also appointed Professor of Greek at University College, Dublin. It was an honour, but it caused him some foreboding, since by now he knew only too well the limits of his strength. In a letter to Newman, he admitted 'weakness and fear' and a feeling of unfitness (*FL*, 63), and he wrote to Bridges of the huge examination load that was to be his responsibility:

I have a salary of £400 a year, but when I first contemplated the six examinations I have yearly to conduct, five of them running, and to the Matriculation there came up last year 750 candidates, I thought that Stephen's Green (the biggest square in Europe) paved with gold would not pay for it. It is an honour and an opening and has many bright sides, but at present it has also some dark ones and this in particular that I am not at all strong, not strong enough for the requirements, and do not see at all how I am to become so. But to talk of weather or health and especially to complain of them is poor work.

(*B*, 190)

His foreboding was to prove all too accurate. Year by year the enormous quantities of papers to be marked weighed upon his spirit. 'It is killing work to examine a nation', he wrote. His letters of these years are punctuated with involuntary gasps and groans, often wryly humorous, but often showing the distress of a man driven beyond his capacity. He wrote to Bridges in October 1886, after spending a summer holiday in Wales:

I was I cannot tell when in such good health and spirits as on my return from Cadwalader and all his goats but 331 accounts of the First Punic War with trimmings, have sweated me down to nearer my lees and usual alluvial low water mudflats, groans, despair, and yearnings.

(*B*, 236)

From one not given to complaining, the distress signs occur with ominous regularity in these years. Perhaps the most poignant comment is one written to Bridges less than a year before his death:

This morning I gave in what I believe is the last batch of examination work for this autumn (and if all were seen, fallen leaves of my poor life between the leaves of it), and but for that want I might prance on ivory this very afternoon. I have had to get glasses, by the bye: just now I cannot be happy either with or without them. The oculist says my sight is very good and my eye perfectly healthy but that like Jane Nightwork I am old.

(*B*, 296)

He was just forty-two at the time, but as he said himself his vitals were grizzled with white hair. Father Lahey makes light of this burden on Hopkins, remarking 'to imagine that a few weeks of distasteful work darkened his whole life is manifestly absurd' (*L*, 140). This might be true if applied to a man of normal constitution, but the weakness and depression to which Hopkins had always been prone, increased during these years. He wrote to Baillie:

The melancholy I have all my life been subject to has become of late years not indeed more intense in its fits but rather more distributed, constant and crippling. One, the lightest but a very inconvenient form of it, is daily anxiety about work to be done, which makes me break off or never finish all that lies outside that work. It is useless to write more on this: when I am at the worst, though my judgment is never affected, my state is much like madness. I see no ground for thinking I shall ever get over it or ever succeed in doing anything that is not forced on me to do of any consequence.

(*FL*, 256)

He embodied his agony in the Sonnets of Desolation which are among his finest creations. They were wrung from him unbidden, without much conscious artifice, and they show a Miltonic sureness and strength of diction. His diaries, what remain of them, also give evidence of his pain, and the dejection and self-loathing he endured.

It is academic to debate whether his torments were an authentic 'dark night of the soul', the final purgation of the mystic before he reaches the bliss of the vision of God. He certainly suffered a crushing deprivation of the mental and physical well-being without which nothing is enjoyable and much is intolerable. His outward circumstances were pleasant enough. He was admittedly a man in exile, a patriotic Englishman in a nationalistic Ireland, but he had plenty of friends, an interesting job, and the opportunity of frequent holidays. But nothing seemed to prosper with him and with despair he realized that he was 'time's eunuch', never to beget.

Both Father Devlin[11] and Dr Pick[12] point out that this impotence and suffering were, in fact, the higher sacrifice that Hopkins had offered to God. He had noted that the keener the consciousness the greater the pain, and had expressed himself willing to be raised to any level of conscious suffering. It was given to him in ample measure, and it is difficult to believe that it was not part of the sanctification he desired. A year before his death he wrote to Bridges:

All impulse fails me: I can give myself no sufficient reason for going on. Nothing comes: I am a eunuch—but it is for the kingdom of heaven's sake. (*B*, 270)

This is a cry of dereliction, but there is, in it, the implicit recognition that his sufferings have some meaning.

It is possible that had Hopkins survived this long period of aridity and darkness he might have emerged into a period of fresh creativity, more mature and more relaxed. The years might have brought a mellowing of his inner conflicts, an abatement of rigour and a consequent release of energy. The Miltonic strength and simplicity of his last sonnets point to the way he might have gone.

But it was not to be. At the beginning of May 1889 he fell ill with fever. It was not severe, and he wrote to his mother of the unexpected rest he was receiving. It worsened, however, and turned out to be typhoid. He was well nursed and happy, and was able to dictate another letter to his mother. During the night of Wednesday, 5 June, however, his condition took a grave turn and his parents were summoned. He now realized he was dying, and on the morning of Saturday, 8 June, he asked for and was given the final blessing and absolution. As he received it, he was heard to say twice or thrice in a low voice, 'I am so happy.'

He then lapsed into total weakness, though as the end approached he seemed to regain a tranquil awareness of his surroundings. At half past one he died peacefully. He was buried in the burial ground of the Society of Jesus at Glasnevin.

The following sober and compassionate words were written of him by a historian of the Jesuit order:

It has been alleged that he ought never to have been a Jesuit; but his love for his order was intense, and we are permitted to believe that, though he had many trials to endure, they were mainly due to his highly wrought temperament. If this be so, it is probable that in other circumstances he would not

[11] *S*, 218–19. Father Devlin adds however that Hopkins may have *presumed beyond his own strength or God's grace.*
[12] *John Pick*, Gerard Manley Hopkins, *pp. 136 et seq. Oxford University Press* (*London, 1942*).

have had a brighter existence, and perhaps would have been deprived of the deepest consolations of his life. But to those who knew Gerard Hopkins his career will always suggest the idea of tragedy. Is this not true of many modern poets? It is consoling that, ... even if a tragic figure, Hopkins has now at long last come into his own.[13]

In the light of the growing attention being paid to both his character and his work, it seems that his true career, even now, has barely begun.

Hopkins and the Art of Rhetoric

Hopkins brought to the English language a new range of techniques to be used in poetry. They are of such variety and sophistication that he has been charged on more than one occasion with being arbitrary and even odd. It is only in the twentieth century, however, that we have come to understand the deep connection between his highly individual linguistic usages and the tensions and exhaustions of his highly charged personality.

Thomas Merton, ex-journalist and critic, now for many years a contemplative monk, wrote some years ago on the correspondence between Hopkins's art and the difficulties of his inner life. Noting the 'sense of technical struggle' which appears in some of Hopkins's poems, he continued:

Hopkins's spiritual struggles fought their way out in problems of rhythm. He made his asceticism bearable by thrusting it over the line into the order of art where he could handle it more objectively. When fortitude became a matter of sprung rhythm, he could keep his sufferings, for the time being, at arm's length.[1]

There is obviously more to be said than this, but it does point to the vital link between Hopkins's life and his art. Problems of order, control, balance and proper expression pressed upon him in both spheres.

It is not surprising then, that rhetoric was a lifelong study with him. Rhetoric is the 'art' of literature, the techniques which can control inspiration when it overflows, sustain it in power when it is weak, and generally give to language its maximum expressiveness. The perfection for which Hopkins struggled in life emerged, in his poetry, in a constant striving for technical perfection. At times the struggle was too naked, and he is 'too finished' as Merton has remarked, in the sense of being subject to a too rigid conscious control by technique. If this is so, it corresponds to the

---

[13] A Page of Irish History. Story of the University College, Dublin, 1883–1909, *compiled by Fathers of the Society of Jesus, 1930, pp. 104–6; extract in B, pp. 319–20.*

[1] The Sign of Jonas, *Hollis and Carter (London, 1953), p. 79.*

lacerating efforts he used to make in life, to flog his tired or rebellious nature into the more perfect service of God, by more prayer, more repentance and more self-denial. Only very late in his life did he learn the value of a little kindness towards himself.[2]

Technique, however, was part of his artistic nature from the beginning, however elaborately he later developed it. The prose of his early journals fairly vibrates and dances with energy, and organizes itself spontaneously into bursts of alliteration and rhyme. The following is a description of a thunderstorm:

Flashes lacing two clouds above or the cloud and the earth started upon the eyes in live veins of rincing or riddling liquid white, inched and jagged as if it were the shivering of a bright riband string which had once been kept bound round a blade, and danced back into its pleatings.

(22 July 1873; *J*, 233)

This passage not only shows the acute and idiosyncratic observation of his prose and verse; it is also the precursor of the controlled violence of such lines as:

Fall, gall themselves, and gash gold vermilion.[3]

His learned researches into rhetoric were a development of this natural tendency. He gathered arts and techniques from Old English poetry, Old Norse and Icelandic verse, Welsh bardic verse and the rhetoric of Greece and Rome.[4] For this we owe him a debt because, despite the elegant finish achieved by Pope and Dryden, the art of English rhetoric had declined since Milton. Three years before his death, Hopkins wrote to Dixon on the poverty of English poetic rhetoric, as distinct from the abundance of its inspiration. He was talking of Wordsworth:

He had a 'divine philosophy' and a lovely gift of verse; but in his work there is nevertheless beaucoup à redire:[5] *it is due to the universal fault in our literature, its weakness is rhetoric. The strictly poetical insight and inspiration of our poetry seems to me to be of the very finest, finer perhaps than the Greek; but its rhetoric is inadequate—seldom firstrate, mostly only just sufficient, sometimes below par. By rhetoric I mean all the common and teachable element in literature, what grammar is to speech, what throughbass is to music, what theatrical experience gives to playwrights.*

(*D*, 141)

Most people could not understand him. Dixon never really understood

---

[2] See '*My own heart let me more have pity on*', p. 163.
[3] '*The Windhover*'.
[4] His '*Lecture Notes on Rhetoric*'—*J*, 267 et seq—show a wide and curious range of learning.
[5] Roughly, '*much that should be done over again*'.

him, and even the admiring and talented Coventry Patmore, himself a poet, was compelled to admit bafflement. Patmore's view is still a commonly-held one:

It seems to me that the thought and feeling of these poems, if expressed without any obscuring novelty of mode, are such as often to require the whole attention to apprehend and digest them; and are therefore of a kind to appeal only to the few. But to the already sufficiently arduous characteristics of such poetry you seem to me to have added the difficulty of following several entirely novel and simultaneous experiments in versification and construction, together with an altogether unprecedented system of alliteration and compound words;—any one of which novelties would be startling and productive of distraction from the poetic matter to be expressed.

(*FL*, 352)

Patmore, unable to believe that Hopkins's style was as native to him as his subject matter, here makes a misleading distinction between 'poetic matter' and 'mode', on the analogy of the contents of a parcel plus its wrapping. It is only perhaps because the twentieth century understands more of the states of mind to which Hopkins was exposed, that it can see the organic connection between these states and the tense taut language in which they found expression. Although in some ways a strict Victorian, Hopkins was, in the deeper aspects of his experience, ahead of his time. He opened up these new dimensions of linguistic usage because he was driven to it by inner pressures.

Sprung Rhythm

Hopkins once said that sprung rhythm simply means 'abrupt' rhythm (*D*, 23). Explaining the matter to Dixon, he said, 'To speak shortly, it consists of scanning by accents or stresses alone, without any account of the number of syllables, so that a foot may be one strong syllable, or it may be many light and one strong' (*D*, 14).

This contrasts with traditional prosody, where the line was built of a number of regular feet. Feet could be disyllabic (iambic ∪–, or trochaic –∪) or trisyllabic (anapaestic ∪∪–, or dactylic –∪∪) but would vary little from line to line. The number of syllables per line was consequently fixed. If a poet decided to write, for example, in iambic pentameters, each line could be expected to contain 5 iambic feet adding up to ten syllables, e.g.

∪   –   ∪   –   ∪   –   ∪   –   ∪   –

The cur | *few tolls* | *the knell* | *of part* | *ing day.*
  1   2   3   4   5

This notation plus the names of the various 'feet' had been imported at

Renaissance times from classical metres. In the classical writers, however, it had referred to the *length* of time a syllable is held, rather than to the *strength of emphasis* put on it—to 'quantity' rather than stress. English, however, is naturally a stressed language, so the notation was unconsciously adapted to mean stress rather than length: e.g. ᴗ– in classical times indicated a 'foot' containing one short and one long syllable: in English prosody it came to mean one unstressed plus one stressed syllable.

The distinction between quantity and stress was not seen very clearly, in theory, before the time of Coleridge. Hopkins, of course, was quite clear about it, saying that 'for simplicity's sake' we could call feet by Greek names, but substitute accent for quantity. In practice, however, the older English poets, notably Donne, the later Shakespeare and the later Milton, had not been straitjacketed by classical metres.

In fact they had used them as basic patterns, but had been very free with the variations on the pattern, e.g. Milton's line

Home to his mother's house private returned

is written to a basic iambic pentameter. To read it as such, however, would make it sound ridiculous, with stresses falling on the wrong syllables. Its proper scansion is the way the reader would speak the words, i.e.

$$— \quad ᴗ \quad ᴗ \quad — \quad ᴗ \quad — \quad — \quad ᴗ \quad ᴗ \quad —$$
Home to | his moth | er's house | private | returned

However, the reader supplies, *with his mind*, the underlying iambic rhythm, on which the actual line is a variation. So a kind of counterpoint is set up, the actual accentual pattern of the line being superimposed upon the iambics running in the reader's mind. However, despite this freedom of stress distribution, the older poets kept to (*a*) a fixed quantity of syllables per line, and (*b*) an *underlying* stress pattern which they would never completely lose.

What Hopkins did was 'professedly' to scrap the idea of a fixed quantity of syllables, and an underlying stress pattern, and allow any number of syllables per line, the unstressed clustering round the stressed. 'For particular rhythmic effects it is allowed, and more freely than in common rhythm, to use *any* number of slack syllables, limited only by the ear' (*D*, 40 [Editor's italics]).

This, however, was not to jettison all form and order. To organize verse written in sprung rhythm, Hopkins adopted the following devices:
1. A fixed number of stresses per line. Even here, however, he made provision for additional stresses demanded by proper pronunciation of the words, calling them '*outriding feet*'. 'An outriding foot', he said 'is, by a sort of contradiction, a recognized extra-metrical effect; it is and it is not part of the metre; not part of it, not being counted, but part of it by producing a

calculated effect which tells in the general success' (*B*, 45). For examples of outriders, see notes on 'The Windhover' and 'Hurrahing in Harvest'.

2. Rhyme—both end of line, and also internal, e.g.

Blue-beating and hoary glow height: or night *still* higher
With belled fire *and the moth-soft Milky Way.*

As well as simple rhyme, Hopkins was a great master of vowel music. In his notebooks he described the subtle beauty that can be given to verse by 'vowelling', 'which is either *vowelling-on* (assonance) or *vowelling-off* i.e. change of vowel down some scale'. Examples of Hopkin's vowel-chimes are:

```
     A   BC  D   E    A        B       E    C   D E  A          E
Her fond yellow hornlight wound to the west, her wild hollow hoarlight hung to the height.
1        2   1   2  34         4 3 1   4 2 1 2   1   2  31         1   3
Waste. . .
4    3
```

These lines combine (*a*) vowel chime (marked above the line), (*b*) four or fivefold alliteration, on several consonants (marked below the line), and (*c*) two chromatic vowel-runs:

fond yellow hornlight/wild hollow hoarlight
and
wound to the west/hung to the height

An example of a simple triumphant run up a vowel scale is:

```
     A      A      B    C     D
Left hand, off land, I hear the lark ascend
1  2   3   4  2 1  4   3      1        4
```

The rising and carolling effect is reinforced by subtle alliterations, and by a heavy initial internal rhyme 'hand/land', the ground from which the song soars.

These vowel effects of rhyme, assonance and chime (vowelling-off) are used in close conjunction with

3. Alliteration. Repetition of consonantal effects. Sometimes Hopkins used it in quite simple fashion, e.g.

This darksome burn, horseback brown
His rollrock highroad roaring down
In coop and in comb the fleece of his foam
Flutes and low to the lake falls home.

Other times, under the influence of Welsh *cynghanedd*[1] he would weave complex patterns of alliteration,e.g.

```
To bathe in his fall-gold mercies, to breathe in his all-fire glances.
1 2        3 4 5 6        1    2      4 3  56
```

The basic idea of sprung rhythm is not new. Hebrew psalmody was

[1] *Pronounced 'kung-hanneth'. See introduction to 'The Sea and the Skylark'.*

organized round a set number of stresses per line with any number of
unstressed syllables in between. The modern renderings set to Gelineau
music reproduce this effect. More to our point, however, Old English
alliterative verse was in sprung rhythm. It had a set number of stresses per
line, each stress clustered with a varying number of non-stressed syllables,
and each line having a number of alliterated consonants. There was no
rhyme, however, and each line was end-stopped, whereas Hopkins used
rhyme, both internal and end-of-line, and also liked to 'overreave' his
verse, not treating the lines as units but running on the scansion from line
to line to the end of the stanza, e.g.

I caught this morning morning's minion, king-
> *dom of daylight's dauphin, dapple-dawn-drawn Falcon, in his*
>> *riding*
> *Of the rolling level underneath him steady air, and striding*
High there,

It is obvious in these lines that both the sense and the metre have to be
carried on from line to line, the effect being to reproduce the continuous
swoop and hurl of the falcon's flight.

To these additional effects, not found in Old English sprung rhythm, but
used by Hopkins one might add that of vowel music. Hopkins had a keen
and subtle ear for music, which he employed occasionally in musical
composition, but chiefly in the rich vocalic texture of his poetry. There is a
magic in his lines, created by use of internal rhyme, assonance, vowel
contrast, chromatic vowel 'runs'. It was a deliberate art which he called
'lettering' and which he regarded as a teachable element in the art of
rhetoric. In the choruses of Euripides where the sound adds another dimension to the meaning, and in the vowel and consonant music of Welsh
cynghanedd Hopkins found his models.

For those who find difficulty in understanding the concept of sprung
rhythm, the principle can be found in some nursery rhymes, as Hopkins
himself pointed out. 'Three Blind Mice', for example, has basically three
stresses per line as follows (stresses in capitals):

	THREE		BLIND		MICE	
	SEE		HOW	*they*	RUN	
They	ALL	*ran*	AF	*ter the*	FAR	*mer's wife,*
She	CUT	*off their*	TAILS	*with a*	CAR	*ving knife,*
Did	EV	*er you*	SEE	*such a*	THING	*in your life*
As	THREE		BLIND		MICE.	

Each line is 'sprung' upon three stresses, with a varying number of
unstressed syllables in between. In the case of words such as 'wife', 'knife'

and 'life', although they are not *metrically* stresses, they can nevertheless receive their full and natural emphasis without disturbing the rhythm of the line. They correspond, to some extent, with what Hopkins called extrametrical or 'outriding' feet: they are adequately accented but not 'counted'. It must be added that Hopkins's poetry cannot be read with a strict 'metronome' pulse as can the nursery rhyme.

There are certain advantages in using sprung rhythm:

Flexibility—not being bound to a fixed number of syllables a poet can get nearer to the natural and sometimes more forcible rhythms of ordinary speech. 'For why, if it is forcible in prose to say "lashed rod", am I obliged to weaken this in verse, which ought to be stronger, not weaker, into "lashed birch-rod" or something?' remarked Hopkins, on the subject of the difficulties imposed by normal metrical usages (*B*, 46, referring to 'The Wreck of the Deutschland', st.2, 1.2).

Rhetorical effect—not bound to an underlying rhythm dictated by a predetermined metre, the poet has far greater freedom to make the sound of his words and phrases enhance his logical meaning. In his note to 'Christabel', in which he used sprung rhythm, Coleridge talked of the new freedom to vary the number of syllables, but added, 'Nevertheless this occasional variation in number of syllables is not introduced wantonly, or for the mere ends of convenience, but in correspondence with some transition, in the nature of the imagery or passion.'

Hopkins himself wrote:

Why do I employ sprung rhythm at all? Because it is the nearest to the rhythm of prose, that is the native and natural rhythm of speech, the least forced, the most rhetorical and emphatic of all possible rhythms, combining, as it seems to me opposite and, one wd. have thought, incompatible excellences, markedness of rhythm—that is rhythm's self—and naturalness of expression . . .

(*B*, 46)

Just after the paragraph quoted above, he insisted, as he did so often, 'My verse is less to be read than heard—it is oratorical.' For to Hopkins, the art of rhetoric—the bringing out of the maximum force and beauty inherent in the sound of spoken language—was paramount. 'Poetry is speech framed to be heard for its own sake and interest even over and above the interest of meaning.'

Hopkins and Duns Scotus

At this time I had first begun to get hold of the copy of Scotus on the Sentences in the Baddely library and was flush with a new stroke of enthusiasm. It

*may come to nothing or it may be a mercy from God. But just then when I took
in any inscape of the sky or sea I thought of Scotus.*
Hopkins, Journal, 1872 (*J*, 221)
Duns Scotus, 1265–1308, was a Franciscan Friar and the greatest British
medieval philosopher. He studied at Oxford and lectured at Paris and
Oxford. He was a great upholder of the doctrine of the Immaculate
Conception of Mary, the mother of Christ. (See note on sonnet 'Duns
Scotus's Oxford'.)

It is his theory of knowledge that concerns us here. He gave to Hopkins a
philosophical justification of the *reality and uniqueness of individual things.*

It had been a feature of the scholastic intellect to discount our knowledge of the particular and individual features of a person or thing—e.g.
the fact that a man might have blue eyes, a crooked nose and a bald
head. These things are perceived by the senses and such knowledge is
precarious compared with the knowledge that this particular man belongs
to the species 'human nature'. It is the intellect, working on sense data
which produces the idea of 'human nature' in general, and it is this
intellectual knowledge of the 'universal' (the thing in general) which is the
only true knowledge to the medieval schoolman.

Reasons for this overemphasis on the reality of abstract knowledge were
possibly these:
1. Since God was conceived of as absolute and undifferentiated Being,
without distinctive parts, it was inevitable that the schoolmen should
think of abstractions as having more 'reality' than particular things,
because they approach nearer to the spiritual and undifferentiated quality
of the (to them) supreme Reality, God.
2. The schoolmen—e.g. St Thomas Aquinas—held that particular things
were only intelligible as being recognized as partaking in general classes.
For example a tree is only recognized as such by the fact of its 'treeness'
or the fact that it belongs to the general category 'tree'. The intellect is
the source of these general categories which alone enable us to make sense
of particulars. The intellect does not know particulars, only general
categories (universals), and therefore there is no 'knowledge' of particular
things.

Scotus replied that the intellect has got a direct, if somewhat confused
knowledge of particular things 'a confused primary intuition of the
particular thing'. The reality of a tree, *this* tree, is not that it partakes in
some abstract idea of tree but that it is a blend of unique qualities (texture,
shape, colour) which give it its individual essence. This essence—which
Scotus termed its '*haecceitas*' meaning 'thisness'—is what constitutes the
reality of the thing.

This was most important to Hopkins. St Thomas, whose authority is great in Catholic philosophy, had denied direct knowledge of particulars, and Hopkins needed a reputable authority for holding otherwise. He needed it because he believed and rejoiced in the myriad particularity of nature, the patterns of particular flowers, cloudscapes and landscapes. He could not bear to think that such knowledge was not direct and real. Everything in nature, to him, is unique and cries out 'What I do is me: for that I came' ('As kingfishers'). In Scotus, 'the Subtle Doctor', he found complete philosophical justification of his view, watertight even against the formidable Aquinas. For this peace of mind and heart he paid tribute to Scotus, the one

... *who of all men most sways my spirits to peace;*
Of realty the rarest-veinèd unraveller: a not
Rivalled insight, be rival Italy or Greece.
('Duns Scotus's Oxford')

Inscape

All the world is full of inscape, and chance left free to act falls into an order as well as purpose.
Hopkins, Journal, 24 February 1873
Basically, 'inscape' to Hopkins meant design or pattern:
... *as air, melody, is what strikes me most of all in music, and design in painting, so design, pattern or what I am in the habit of calling 'inscape' is what I above all aim at in poetry.*
(*B*, 66)

Nature full of inscape
The wonder of nature, to Hopkins, was that it is a never-ending source of inscapes—patterns of shape, sound, light and colour, revealing the infinite energies of God. 'Unless you refresh the mind from time to time', he wrote to Dixon, 'you cannot always remember or believe how deep the inscape in things is' (*D*, 135). The myriad forms of nature are all unique, separately inscaped by God. Each thing, from the lowest piece of inanimate matter to the most 'highly pitched, selved and distinctive' thing in creation, the mind of man, has its own inscape, which gives it its own 'self' or identity.

The inscaping mind
The mind of man is unique, in that it can both create inscapes—in stone, paint, words, sound—and also recognize the infinite inscapes of nature.

Art and religion here meet, for Hopkins, because man can give praise to God for the whole created world.

Variety of inscape is endless, for the mind of each man is unique, separately inscaped by the Creator. Men live in a common world, but they inscape it separately according to their individual modes of awareness. The city of Oxford, Hopkins once said, is beautiful for all men but, apart from her public beauty, she has a private or 'byeways' beauty for each individual. (Early poem 'To Oxford'.)

Inscape and the mind of Gerard Manley Hopkins

Hopkins's mind, with its intensity and idiosyncrasy, constantly strove to find patterns and perspectives in nature, to 'law out the shapes' and designs in all things. He looks, for instance, at breakers on the shore and tries to find a true perspective. A careful description is followed by this confession that he has failed to find the true inscape of the scene:

About all the turns of the scaping from the break and flooding of the wave to its run out again I have not yet satisfied myself. The shores are swimming and the eyes have before them a region of milky surf but it is hard for them to unpack the huddling and gnarls of the water and law out the shapes and sequence of the running.

(*J*, 164)

His Journal is full of descriptions of things, looked at from a personal and sometimes peculiar angle. He strove always to inscape nature thus, and one finds him wrestling with words to impart exactly what he has seen:

A fine sunset: the higher sky dead clear blue bridged by a broad slant causeway rising from right to left of wisped or grass cloud, the wisps lying across: the sundown yellow, moist with light but ending at the top in a foam of delicate white pearling and spotted with big tufts of cloud in colour russet between brown and purple but edged with brassy light. But what I note it all for is this: before, I had always taken the sunset and the sun as quite out of gauge with each other, as indeed physically they are, for the eye after looking at the sun is blunted to everything else and if you look at the rest of the sunset you must cover the sun, but today I inscaped them together and made the sun the true eye and ace of the whole, as it is. It was all active and tossing out light and started as strongly forward from the field as a long stone or a boss in the knop of the chalice-stem: it is indeed by stalling[1] *it so that it falls into scape with the sky.*

(*J*, 196 [Editor's roman])

This wrestling with words to inscape a scene in prose is raised to further

[1]stalling—*organizing it in the mind.*

intensity in his poetry, where he is striving to inscape his sound patterns as well as his logical meaning. Hence the tendency, at times, to become 'queer': *Now it is the virtue of design, pattern, or inscape to be distinctive and it is the vice of distinctiveness to become queer. This vice I cannot have escaped.* (*B*, 66)

Inscape 'the very soul of art'

Art, to Hopkins, was nothing at all to do with the reproduction of surface reality. It has to do with the 'shape' or pattern imposed by the artist on his raw material—paint, words, stone, etc. It is the shape itself that matters, not its correspondence to anything outside itself.

His final judgment, for instance, on a picture by Holman Hunt is that 'it has no inscape of composition whatever'. He means that the picture is 'bitty', lacking in unity of vision. Instead of shaping his colours and perspectives to his inner vision, Hunt appears to have been content to produce a copy of surface reality. 'Inscape', continued Hopkins, 'could scarcely bear up against such realism.'

Conversely he praised another picture where the artist had tried to express his vision of the sitter's inner character: 'Intense expression of face, expression of character, not mood, true inscape—I think it could hardly be exceeded' (*J*, 245).

Inscaping in art, to Hopkins, involved the shaping, even the distorting of material, in the interests of artistic purpose. Scapeless art, to him, was aimless art. This view lies behind his remark that inscape is the very soul of art.

The inscape of poetry

Some of Hopkins's most important revealing utterances on poetry are to be found in his Lecture Notes on Rhetoric. In one place he defines poetry as 'speech framed to be heard for its own sake and interest even over and above the interest of meaning' (*J*, 289).

Writing to Coventry Patmore, he spoke of the many merits and the ultimate deficiency of an Irish poet, Sir Samuel Ferguson, as follows: *... he was a poet as the Irish are ... full of feeling, high thoughts, flow of verse, point, often fine imagery and other virtues, but the essential and only lasting thing left out—what I call* inscape, *that is species or individually-distinctive beauty of style.* (*FL*, 373)

It is what he calls 'the shape' that matters. Poetry is to him a pattern of sound, and the 'shape' or 'inscape' of the speech–sound is more important than the logical content. 'Some matter or meaning is essential to it but only as an element necessary to support and employ the shape which is contemplated for its own sake' (ibid.). The 'shape' is the total sound pattern of the spoken poem as received by the hearing ear and contemplated by the listening mind.

This is not to say that Hopkins abandoned logical sense—he was the last one to do this—but he was always willing to sacrifice immediate intelligibility in the interests of inscaping or designing the sound. Poetry to him stood halfway between prose and music. Prose carries logical meaning through grammar and syntax. Music communicates another kind of meaning through patterns of sound, non-verbal. Poetry to Hopkins was neither prose nor music—it uses the spoken word, not for the same purposes as prose uses it, but to create a pattern of speech-sound. 'Poetry is in fact speech only employed to carry the inscape of speech *for the inscape's sake*' (ibid.—Editor's italics).

Hence his intense preoccupation with rhythm, alliteration, assonance, *cynghanedd* and the whole art of what he called 'lettering'[2] the syllables. These are the devices which turn mere speech into patterns of pleasurable sound, the means by which speech-sound is inscaped. Hence, too, his syntactical difficulty and occasional eccentricity. In the light of a clear understanding of what Hopkins was trying to do with poetry, these latter are not such obstacles after all.

Some of the more obvious devices Hopkins used to inscape his language are as follows. Most of them have the effect of turning a merely logical sequence of words into a sculpted pattern of sound and sense.

Compound adjectives
These are almost invariably coupled with alliteration and/or internal rhyme.
dappled-with-damson-west
('The Wreck of the Deutschland', st. 5)
sodden-with-its-sorrowing heart
(ibid., st. 27)
dapple-dawn-drawn Falcon
('The Windhover')
tumbled over rim in roundy wells / Stones
('As kingfishers catch fire, dragonflies draw flame')
O-seal-that-so feature
('To What Serves Mortal Beauty?')

[2] *'Lettering'—Hopkins treated the subject, at length, in his Lecture Notes on Rhetoric (**J**, 283).*

Inversions of word-order
Death or distance soon consumes them: **wind**
What most I may eye after, . . .
('The Lantern out of Doors')
Now Time's Andromeda on this rock rude,
With not her either beauty's equal or
Her injury's . . .
('Andromeda')
When will you ever, Peace, wild wooddove, shy wings shut,
Your round me roaming end, *and* **under be my boughs ?**
When, when, Peace, will you Peace? I'll not play hypocrite
To own my heart: . . .
('Peace')
How far from then forethought of, *all thy more boisterous years,*
('Felix Randal')

> *. . . cliffs of fall*
Frightful, sheer, no-man-fathomed. **Hold them cheap**
May who ne'er hung there . . .
('No worst, there is none')

> *. . . feel*
That ne'er need hunger, *Tom; . . .*
('Tom's Garland')

Compression and ellipsis
This is usually accompanied by inversion of word-order.
   Hopkins frequently omits relative pronouns. The examples given—and complained about—by Bridges are:
Squander the hell-rook ranks sally to molest him'
('The Bugler's First Communion')
meaning 'Scatter the hell-sent squadrons *that* sally forth to molest him'
and
'O Hero savest' for 'O Hero *that* savest'
('The Loss of the Eurydice')
He also omits, at times, other particles, such as prepositions, e.g.
'Some candle clear burns somewhere I come by'
for 'Some candle clear burns somewhere *as* I come by'.
   The reason for these omissions or ellipses is that Hopkins wished to cut out as far as possible all merely toneless and grammatical elements in his verse.
   Other examples of compression and ellipsis, apart from single-word instances like *'Fire-featuring heaven'* ('Spelt from Sibyl's Leaves') and

'yestertempests's creases' ('That Nature is a Heraclitean Fire') are:
Or to-fro tender trambeams truckle at the eye.
('The Candle Indoors')
Forward-like, but however, and like favourable heaven heard these.
('The Bugler's First Communion')
                              . . . flung prouder form
Than Purcell tune lets tread to? . . .
('To What Serves Mortal Beauty')
                              . . . the heart,
Since, proud, it calls the calling manly, gives a guess
That, hopes that, makesbelieve, the men must be no less;
('The Soldier')
      I cast for comfort I can no more get
By groping round my comfortless, than blind
Eyes in their dark can day . . .
('My own heart let me more have pity on')

Miscellaneous
The following, for the most part, are pure felicities of language, exemplifying Hopkins's dictum that poetry is 'speech framed to be heard for its own sake and interest'. Logical content is only one element and not necessarily the primary one. 'Some matter or meaning is essential to it', he said, 'but only as an element necessary to support and employ the shape which is contemplated for its own sake' (see p. 24). Most of these examples show a daring use of the associative power of words, allied to complex sound effects produced by alliteration and internal rhyme.

O Father, not under thy feathers nor ever as guessing
The goal was a shoal, of a fourth the doom to be drowned;
('The Wreck of the Deutschland', st. 12)
The grey lawns cold where gold, where quickgold, lies!
('The Starlight Night')
March, kind comrade, abreast him;
Dress his days to a dexterous and starlight order.
('The Bugler's First Communion')
           . . . nor spare a sigh
Though worlds of wanwood leafmeal lie;
('Spring and Fall')
           . . . This to hoard unheard,
Heard unheeded, leaves me a lonely began.
('To seem the stranger lies my lot, my life')

Nine months she then, nay years, nine years she long
Within her wears, bears, cares and combs the same:
('To R.B.')

A detailed analysis of some of Hopkins's syntactical usages is to be found in *Gerard Manley Hopkins* by W. A. M. Peters, S.J. (Oxford University Press, 1948).

Instress
The word 'instress' is used by Hopkins with subtle shiftings of meaning: it is occasionally interchangeable with 'inscape', but usually distinct. The main meanings appear to be as follows:

Instress as shaping energy
Discussing the early Greek philosopher Parmenides, Hopkins interprets him as meaning 'that all things are upheld by instress and meaningless without it' (*J*, 127). Whether Hopkins is right or not about Parmenides, the statement illumines one aspect of instress as the undercurrent of creative energy that supports and binds together the whole of the created world giving things shape, form and meaning to the eye of the beholder. Without this current of instress which runs alike through the outside world and through the perceiving mind there would be no 'bridge' between the two, and the world would be unintelligible:
There would be no bridge, no stem of stress between us and things to bear
us out and carry the mind over.
(ibid.)

To experience directly the instress of nature, demands intense and solitary contemplation. One day, walking on the fells with a companion, Hopkins perceived the design of the long grasses: 'Green-white tufts of long bleached grass like the heads of hair, each a whorl of slender curves, one tuft taking up another.' However, although he had found the in*scape*, the in*stress* eluded him—'with a companion the eye and the ear are for the most part shut, and instress cannot come' (*J*, 228). The poem 'Hurrahing in Harvest' describes a moment of ecstasy when the poet experiences the instress of nature, the divine energy that fills all things.
These things, these things were here and but the beholder
    Wanting; which two when they once meet,
The heart rears wings bold and bolder
    And hurls for him, O half hurls earth for him off under his feet.

Instress in art
Instress in art is the continuity and pressure of vision which binds and

organizes every detail of a work of art to the artist's vision. All the details of a medieval cathedral, for example, though the work of many hands, seem to be instressed by a common vision.

Commenting on the Lady Chapel at Ely, Hopkins wrote that it 'has its walls bordered all round with an ogee-canopied arcade of great richness. . . . The all-powerfulness of instress in mode and the immediateness of its effect are very remarkable' (*J*, 188).

The instressing mind

Hopkins sometimes attached the word 'instress' to the network of association and feeling evoked in him by certain scenes or works of art. Writing to Robert Bridges of a Dorset poet called Barnes, Hopkins said:

His poems use to charm me also by their Westcountry 'instress', a most peculiar product of England, which I associate with airs like Weeping Winefred, Polly Oliver, or Poor Mary Ann, with Herrick and Herbert, with the Worcestershire, Herefordshire, and Welsh landscape, and above all with the smell of oxeyes and applelofts: this instress is helped by particular rhythms and these Barnes employs.
(*B*, 88)

Summary

Instress is the underlying energy that organizes nature into pattern and unity—it runs also through the human mind (which is part of nature) enabling it to make sense of the world. It underlies all particular inscapes as the total life and personality of the artist lies behind any particular work of art he may produce.

By contemplation of simple objects—flowers, trees, streams and landscapes—Hopkins was at times raised to ecstasy, because he realized that the hidden energy (instress) moulding things into shapes, patterns and colours (inscapes) was the very energy of God himself. This outward and visible beauty was to him the reflection of the energy and invisible beauty of God. So in this sense all nature was sacramental to him—the visible sign of an invisible, intelligent and creative energy.

Commentary

The Wreck of the Deutschland

Hopkins wrote 'The Wreck of the Deutschland' in 1875 at the age of thirty-one while studying philosophy at St Beuno's College in North Wales. He had written nothing for several years since he had become a Jesuit, having resolved, as he wrote to Dixon, 'to write no more as not belonging to my profession, unless it were by the wish of my superiors' (*D*, 14).

It is his major, if not his best, poem and it has been much misunderstood. The Jesuit magazine *The Month* refused it, and even his friend Bridges, judging by a later remark of Hopkins himself, must have written to him to say that he would not for any money read the poem again. Bridges's adverse criticism drew a half-amused, half-hurt protest from Hopkins:

our first criticisms are not our truest, best, most homefelt, or most lasting but what comes easiest on the instant. They are barbarous and like what the ignorant and the ruck say. This was so with you. The Deutschland on her first run worked very much and unsettled you, thickening and clouding your mind with vulgar mudbottom and common sewage (I see that I am going it with the image) and just then unhappily you drew off your criticisms all stinking.
(*B*, 50)

The amiable Dixon was kinder, as usual, if somewhat guarded:

the Deutschland is enormously powerful: if has however such elements of deep distress in it that one reads it with less excited delight, though not with less interest than the others. I hope that you will accept the tribute of my deep and intense admiration.
(*D*, 32–3)

Hopkins defended himself. His first plea, as ever, was the strictly oratorical nature of his verse:

My verse is less to be read than heard as I have told you before: it is oratorical, that is the rhythm is so. I think if you will study what I have here said you will be much more pleased with it and, may I say? converted to it.
(*B*, 46)

On Bridges's charge of obscurity, he answered:

Granted that it needs study and is obscure, for indeed I was not over desirous that the meaning of all should be quite clear, at least unmistakable, you might, without the effort that to make it all out would seem to have required, have nevertheless read it so that lines and stanzas should be left in the memory and superficial impressions deepened, and have liked some without exhausting all. I am sure I have read and enjoyed pages of poetry that way.
(*B*, 50)

He concluded that he would not think of altering anything because he did not write for the public. 'You are my public and I hope to convert you', he wrote to Bridges. Bridges never was converted: he called it 'a great dragon folded at the gate to forbid all entrance.' (Notes to his edition of Hopkins's poems).

It was Hopkins's first experiment with sprung rhythm.[1] In the years of his poetic silence this new rhythm had grown in his mind. He wrote to Dixon: *I had long had haunting my ear the echo of a new rhythm which I now realized on paper. To speak shortly, it consists in scanning by accents or stress alone, without any account of the number of syllables, so that a foot may be one strong syllable, or it may be many light and one strong.*
(*D*, 14)
It seemed to him that sprung rhythm was 'a better and more natural principle than the ordinary system, much more flexible and capable of much greater effects'.

It says much for Father Coleridge, the editor of *The Month* that he accepted the poem at all, even though he did not subsequently print it. It must have struck him as wildly eccentric. The stresses marked, sometimes arbitrarily, in blue chalk, the rhymes carried on from one line to the other,[2] the patterned chiming of vowel and consonant derived from the ancient and sophisticated Welsh tradition of *cynghanedd*;[3] these, plus what Hopkins himself admitted to be 'a great many more oddnesses', would have dismayed the most avant-garde of editors.

When writing this commentary on 'The Wreck of the Deutschland', certain remarks of Hopkins's about total explanation being neither desirable nor possible have been held in mind. This poem is an ode, not a narrative piece. 'The principal business is lyrical' as in the odes of Pindar, and the rich emotional effects are achieved by the use of multi-valued words and phrases which allow a number of merely logical explanations; also by a complex play of consonant and vowel, where sound rather than sense is paramount. It would therefore be misguided to ask for, or to offer, a one-to-one rational explanation. One can merely point to the effects, and to the techniques and intentions underlying them.

Some readers may find the poem somewhat off-putting because of its ultamontane Catholicism, its dogmatic fervour in praise of the Virgin Mary[4] and of Catholic saints and martyrs, together with its general intolerance of all non-Catholic religious outlooks.[5] Bridges in fact accused

---

[1] *See Introduction, p. 16.*
[2] *e.g. St. 27, 11.7–8; st. 31, 11.3–4 and 6–7.*
[3] *e.g. St. 8, 11.3–4.*
[4] *e.g. St. 34.*
[5] *e.g. St. 20.*

Hopkins of forcing emotion into religious channels[6] implying that the strength of feeling displayed in Hopkins's words was not in fact really present.

To this, it may be said that Hopkins was, to the last, one of the generation of the Oxford Movement of the mid nineteenth century—fervent, intellectual, High Church, thirsting for dogma and liturgy and above all for authority in religious matters. This authority he found, in full, in the Roman Catholic Church as she was at the time, still rigid in her counter-Reformation outlook, binding her faithful to her by infallible decree and uncompromising ordinance.

Both by circumstance then, but also by psychological necessity was Hopkins a Catholic of the authoritarian kind, his will bent on humility and obedience to an omnipotent God,[7] whose presence he strove to discern in all things—in beauty and terror of the world, in the consolations and paralysing desolations of his own inner life,[8] and above all in the liturgy and dogma of the Church. For some people, he wrote, the Church's dogma, e.g. the Trinity, is 'the dull algebra of schoolmen'. To others, it is the breath of life.

... news of their dearest friend or friends, leaving them all their lives balancing whether they have three heavenly friends or one—not that they have any doubt on the subject, but that their knowledge leaves their minds swinging: poised but on the quiver. And this might be the ecstasy of interest, one would think.

(*B*, 187–8)

As far as Bridges's accusation is concerned, if there is any forcing of feeling into religious channels in this poem it is the reflection of something native to the personality of Hopkins: the naked fervour of will with which he clung to faith and obedience, sometimes aided by his natural feelings but often in the teeth of depression and spiritual aridity that made a wasteland of his inner self.[9] Moreover he wrote it in the midst of a religious training which steels the will, sharpens the vision and calls forth the utmost in love and self-dedication to Christ.

Our more psychologically minded age has sometimes discerned much danger in Hopkins's total suppression of a normal emotional life, and has

[6] *Preface to Notes (First Edition). Section on 'Mannerism'.*
[7] *'So God as our sovereign has only one will and that will we ought to do and to do it is to love him; it is willingly to obey him, and this willing obedience is divine charity.' (Sermon, 1880. S, 52.)*
[8] *See the Sonnets of Desolation, especially 'Carrion Comfort'.*
[9] *See note on st. 1 of 'The Wreck of the Deutschland'; also 'Carrion Comfort'. According to Father Devlin, S.J., Hopkins overdid the distinction between the will and the feelings (S, 118).*

diagnosed irrational fears and compulsions behind his religious fervour. Even if this were true,[10] it would still have to be said (*a*) that, given his difficult and arduous personality, the religious path was probably the only one for him; (*b*) that the extreme tensions of his personality begat his distinctive style; and (*c*) that he was consistent to the end in his faith and he died happy.

In the last analysis, however, one does not have to accept Hopkins's beliefs, one has only to understand them. The ecstatic play of sound and rhythm, and the odd intensity of word and image convey an experience far beyond the mere transmission of some dogmatic statement. Those who do not share his beliefs may, nevertheless, through his language, experience the rapt moods of fear and contemplation which he seeks to convey. The principal business is lyrical.

Part the First

Stanza 1
There is a slow, tolling rhythm about this first stanza suggesting the death knell and the fear of God.
mastering-me (line 1): used as adjective, cf. Pindar, 'God the all-things-creating-for-men'.
sway (line 3): possibly 2 senses: (1) God as being the sway (surge) of the ocean, and (2) as holding sway (command) over it. Cf. st. 32, ll. 3-4.
bound (line 5): made, created.
fastened me flesh (line 5): formed flesh (in) me. Cf. Job x, 11.
almost unmade (line 6): Hopkins was subject to attacks of nervous derangement, when mind and body seemed to him almost unhinged. He saw in these visitations the dark and terrible side of God's love—cf. (Carrion Comfort) (p. 150). He describes one attack as follows:
nature in all her parcels and faculties gaped and fell apart fatiscebat, *like a clod cleaving and holding only by strings of root. But this must often be.*
(*J*, 16 August 1873) Cf. Job, x, 8.
Over again I feel thy finger (line 8): here, as later with 'The Loss of the Euridyce', Hopkins is moved by a shipwreck report, seeing in it an outward manifestation of this dark Providence. Shipwreck is an adequate embodiment or 'objective correlative' of the inner state described, e.g. in 'No worst, there is none'—hence possibly the continuing fascination of the subject for Hopkins. Much of this poem is a projection of the poet himself, as one might expect in an Ode—cf. Milton's 'Lycidas'.

---

[10] *Some parts of Hopkins's private papers have been expunged or destroyed.*

Stanza 2

lashed rod (line 2): always a toughness about Hopkins, despite frail physique.

He records casually how as a senior boy at school he argued with the unjust Head, who lashed at him wildly with a riding crop. (Letter to Luxmoore, 7 May 1862.)

Thou knowest, etc. (line 5): still addressing God. He relates here and in next stanza, a frightening mystical experience probably also the subject of 'Carrion Comfort'. 'What refers to myself in the poem is all strictly and literally true and did all occur' (*B*, 47). The experience referred to here is almost certainly related to an entry in Hopkins's Journal, 18 September 1873:

I had a nightmare that night. I thought something or someone leapt onto me and held me quite fast; this I think woke me, so that after this I shall have had the use of reason. This first start is, I think, a nervous collapse of the same sort as when one is very tired and holding oneself at stress not to sleep yet suddenly goes slack and seems to fall and wakes, only on a greater scale and with a loss of muscular control reaching more or less deep; this one to the chest and not further, so that I could speak, whispering at first, then louder. . . . The feeling is terrible: the body no longer swayed as a piece by the nervous and muscular instress seems to fall in and hang like a dead weight on the chest. I cried on the holy name and by degrees recovered myself as I thought to do. It made me think that this was how the souls in hell would be imprisoned in their bodies as in prisons.

(*J*, 238)

midriff astrain (line 8): odd expression, but clear enough to convey the muscular tension of extreme inner stress and fear.

leaning of . . . stress (line 8): syntax is 'Midriff, astrain with the pressure of and pierced with the fire of the overwhelming experience'.

Stanza 3

the hurtle of hell (line 2): the mind has 'cliffs of fall, frightful, sheer, no man-fathomed' (Sonnet 'No worst, there is none').

a place (line 3): i.e. of refuge from the terror.

I whirled out wings that spell (line 4): 'I cried on the holy name and by degrees recovered myself.' (See quotation above.)

heart of the Host (line 5): the presence of Christ in the 'Host', the bread in the Tabernacle. Since Hopkins was at St Beuno's at the time, the Host would not be far away from him.

My heart, etc. (line 6): He compliments his heart as being 'dovewinged' (swift and loving) and 'carrier-witted' (having an instinct for 'home', in this case Christ in the Host).

from the flame to the flame (line 8): this, and the parallel 'grace to the grace', imply that God was present both in the terror which his human frailty could not stand and in the comforting Host to which he was forced, in heart, to flee.

Stanza 4

A reflection on his inner precariousness, secured only by Christ.

soft sift (line 1): sand

hourglass (line 2): shaped like a large egg-timer, sand trickling through a narrow neck in the glass.

Todd K. Bender points to some lines of George Herbert (beloved of Hopkins), associating mortal flesh with an hourglass:

> *... thou mayst know*
> *That flesh is but the glass, which holds the dust*
> *That measures all our time; which also shall*
> *Be crumbled into dust ...*

('Church Monuments', quoted by Todd K. Bender in *Gerard Manley Hopkins*, The Classical Background and Critical Reception of His Work Johns Hopkins Press / Oxford University Press, 1966, pp. 87–8)

at the wall | Fast, but mined with a motion (lines 2–3): the sand remains high at the edges but drains at the middle, an image to Hopkins of mortality in general constantly tending towards death, and of himself in particular, subject to feelings of inner disintegration. 'A purpose may look smooth and perfect from without but be frayed and faltering from within', he wrote (*D*, 88).

I steady (line 5): verb, come to rest.

poise (line 5): equilibrium.

pane (line 5): smooth surface; also a lock in an irrigation system that holds the water at a steady level.

roped with (line 6): supported by.

voel (line 7): (Welsh) mountain. To Hopkins 'mind has mountains' (see 'No worst').

vein (line 7): aspect, facet, part. Suggestion of many rich veins in the 'gospel proffer'.

proffer (line 8): a noun meaning promise/offer in the 'gospel' of Christ.

pressure (line 8): revelation, confrontation, demand.

Christ's gift (line 8): possibly of Himself in Communion, but more likely in apposition to 'gospel proffer'.

A paraphrase of lines 5–8 of this stanza might run as follows:

I come to rest like water in a well, to equilibrium, to smoothness,
Provided that I am constantly replenished, nourished, supported

From the heights above, by some revelation, some truth, from
The riches of the gospel, Christ's gift.
'Roped with' is *also* a metaphor from mountain climbing. Hopkins often
had to cling to God, like a climber to a cliffside, when his inner life became
precarious.

Stanza 5
wafting him out of it (line 3): a gesture of affection to him (Christ) whose
face *is* the 'lovely-asunder/Starlight'.
dappled-with-damson (line 5): streaked with purple. Hopkins's Journal is
full of minute descriptions of sunset effects.
Since, tho', etc. (line 6): the general sense is that, although God is perpetually present in created nature, His presence in it must be 'instressed'
(perceived, intensified, clarified) and 'stressed' (proclaimed) by human
beings. This idea is fully developed in the last lines of 'Hurrahing in
Harvest'.
For I greet him, etc. (line 8): whenever the poet experiences the presence
of God in nature he makes some outward and conscious gesture of
acknowledgment. Hopkins regarded this giving of conscious glory to God
as man's unique privilege.

Stanzas 6–9

These stanzas are difficult but important. Hopkins is saying that God's
fullest and most demanding revelation to man is not in beauties or disasters
of nature, but in Christ's suffering and death. The latter, though a single
historical action, is nevertheless perpetuated in time, through the human
sufferings of those who compose His mystical body on earth. It is in this
framework that he is to interpret the sufferings of the nuns on the
Deutschland.

Stanza 6
Paraphrase of lines 1–6: 'Not in his "bliss" (His presence in the peace
and beauty of nature) is the real "stress" (revelation, encounter with,
demand upon, man) of God. Nor even in those disasters of nature—not
sent direct from God despite common opinion to the contrary—though
these can move guilty hearts to repentance and (hard?) hearts to tears.'
But it (line 7): i.e. the 'stress felt'.
rides time, etc. (line 7): is forever present and active in the flow of time.
And here (line 8): i.e. at this point. Hopkins is remarking that what he is

about to say is hard for the faithful and incomprehensible to those of no faith.

Stanza 7

It (line 1): still the 'stress' as explained in notes on stanza 6.

Warm-laid grave of a womb-life grey (line 3): possibly the Incarnation. More likely the Resurrection when Christ led humanity, through death to new life, thus ending the 'womb-life' (the merely natural life) and inaugurating a new era (Rom. vi, 3–6).

Passion (line 5): Latin *passio*, the name traditionally given to the sufferings of Christ before His death.

frightful sweat (line 5): Christ sweated blood at Gethsemane (Luke, xxii, 44).

Thence the discharge of it (line 6): Hopkins frequently uses electrical metaphors to convey God's presence in the world. Christ was the fullest 'discharge' of God's love upon the world. In a meditation written long afterwards in 1884, Hopkins wrote: 'The piercing of Christ's side. The sacred body and the sacred heart seemed waiting for an opportunity of discharging themselves and testifying their total devotion of themselves to the cause of man' (*S*, 255).

swelling (line 6): an image developed in stanza 8.

Though felt before (line 7): Christ was prefigured in Old Testament history and prophecy.

in high flood yet (line 7): in the sense that Christ's life and death are re-enacted daily, sacramentally in the Mass and mystically in the sufferings of Christians (Col., i, 24).

Stanza 8

The peculiar image of the sloe, his 'best or worst word' on the last (final) Word of God, i.e. Christ.

lush-kept, plush-capped (line 3): an image of ripeness; Christ came in the fullness of time. Tenderness of flesh—see below.

sloe (line 3): a wild bitter plum growing on a blackthorn, but here qualified with 'lush-kept, plush-capped', which suggest ripe sweetness and human cultivation. It is used here as an image of Christ's body on the Cross, a bitter-sweet fruit on a bitter tree, and it has the following associations, all to be found in the ancient Good Friday hymn, '*Crux Fidelis*'.

mouthed to flesh-burst (line 4): (when) bitten till its flesh is pierced. Lines in '*Crux Fidelis*' are:

Nails his tender flesh are rending
See his side is opened now

Gush!—flush the man (line 5): Christ's blood was poured on the world.
Cf. '*Crux Fidelis*'
   . . . to cleanse the whole creation
   Streams of blood and water flow.
(See also *S*, 255; 21 March 1884.)
sour or sweet (line 5): possibly in apposition to 'man'. More likely
adverbial to 'flush'. Refers to the compelling pungency of the sloe whether
sour or sweet and, by implication, to the impact of Christ on men.
Hither then, etc. (line 6): men, whether they want to be or not, are still
drawn to this 'hero', and to His Cross.

Stanzas 9–10

Stanzas 9–10 are the last two stanzas of Part the First. Hopkins recom-
mended to the unsympathetic and uncomprehending Bridges that he
might at least read these two stanzas as being easier than the rest.

Stanza 9
lines 1–4: similar in tone to Donne's famous sonnet:
'Batter my heart, three-personed God'.
lines 5–8: Hopkins pursues the theme of the mixed sweetness and bitterness of God's love through a series of paradoxes. God is lightning yet also
love, a winter yet warm, and a comforter of the heart He himself has
crushed.

Stanza 10
A plea to God to have His will with all men either swiftly ('With an anvil-
ding/And with fire') as with Paul (Acts, vi, 1–6), or gradually ('stealing
as Spring') as with St Augustine.

Part the Second

A lyrical narrative of the sinking of the Deutschland. Hopkins obtained
the details from reports in *The Times*.

Stanza 11
This opening stanza is a meditation on man's heedlessness of his last end.
goes Death (line 3): i.e. cries Death, hence inverted commas.
Wave with the meadow (line 7): enjoy life heedlessly.
there (line 7): i.e. in that 'meadow' of life.
scythe (line 8): time and death traditionally personified as a reaper with a
scythe.

cringe (line 8): cause to cringe.

share (line 8): ploughshare, overturning and burying the meadow.

Stanza 12

American-outward-bound (line 2): the Deutschland had started from Bremen and was due to touch at Southampton before proceeding to America.

not under thy feathers (line 5): not consciously committed to God.

The goal was a shoal (line 6): (that) the end of the voyage was to be an outcrop of sand.

of a fourth, etc. (line 6): the syntax is—'nor guessing that it was to be the fate of a quarter to be drowned.'

lines 7–8: God's mercy, albeit the dark and mysterious side, was present.

Stanza 13

regular blow (line 5): ceaseless wind.

in cursed quarter (line 6): the wind, blowing from east-north-east, forced the ship on to a westerly course to avoid the shoals off the Dutch coast, with the result that she was blown on to the Thames shoals.

Wiry (line 7): the sound of the word is right in the context. Logical meaning (of secondary importance) is 'violently driven in spirals'. Cf. 'Home-coiling wiry bushes of spray' (Journal, 20 April 1874).

Stanza 14

combs (line 3): ridges.

Kentish Knock (line 4): a large shoal at the mouth of the Thames, twenty-three miles east of Harwich.

whorl (line 7): propeller. The Deutschland was a screw steamship.

wind (line 8): steer.

Stanza 15

lines 1–2: a slight variation in the rhythm to embody the deepening of the foreboding. The lines are of 3 stresses as usual, but with an unusually emphatic stress on the first syllable.

And frightful a nightfall (line 5): a richly wrought line compounded of:
Alliteration—f–l/f–ll/f–ld/f–l–d. Internal rhyme and half rhyme:

ful—fall—fold—ful.

fright—night.

See note on *cynghanedd* (pp. 18 and 63).

To the shrouds they took (line 8): *The Times* reported, 'Most of the crew and many of the emigrants went into the rigging where they were safe enough as long as they could maintain their hold. But the intense cold and long exposure told a tale.' (*FL*, 442)

Stanza 16
One stirred, etc. (line 1): *The Times* reported this incident as follows: 'One brave sailor who was safe in the rigging went down to try and save a child or woman who was drowning on deck. He was secured by a rope to the rigging but a wave dashed him against the bulwarks, and when daylight dawned his headless body, detained by the rope, was seen swaying to and fro with the waves.'
(ibid.)
tell (line 6): see.
cobbled (line 7): alliterates with 'could'.
burl (line 8): literally 'spin'. Here conveys both sound and movement.
buck and flood (line 8): the sound echoes the impact and flood of the wave.

Stanza 17
line 3: the jarring and elliptical syntax helps convey the chaos of the scene, as people in the rigging, numbed with cold, began to fall on to the deck or into the water. A report in *The Illustrated London News* mentions this scene (see *FL*, 441).
Night roared (line 5): night itself, depicted here as crying with heartbreak. 'The shrieks and sobbing of the women and children are described by the survivors as agonizing' (*The Times*)'
A prophetess towered (line 8): *The Times* described how the five nuns clasped hands and were drowned together 'the chief sister, a gaunt woman 6ft high, calling out loudly and often "O Christ come quickly", till the end came' (*FL*, 443).

Stanza 18
A lyrical pause in the narrative. The poet has been touched to tears and to 'glee' (joy) by the thought of the nun's faith before death.
you (line 2): he affectionately cross-questions his own heart, which, even though 'unteachably after evil' (cf. Jer., xvii, 9) is nevertheless the 'mother of being' in him and a medium of truth.
madrigal (line 6): used here as an adjective meaning sweet or happy.
start (line 6): impulse.
Never-eldering, etc. (line 7): a remarkable line, beautiful in sound and image, referring to his heart.

Stanza 19
master (line 2): i.e. Christ.
Hawling (line 3): howling/hauling/brawling.
rash (line 4): sweeping headlong.
smart (line 4): stinging.
sloggering (line 4): suggests violence, also wetness.
she that weather (line 5): she, (in) that weather.
fetch (line 6): purpose, focus of attention.
rode over (line 8): according to another dramatic report the tall nun, standing on a table below decks, thrust her body through a skylight 'and kept exclaiming in a voice heard by those in the rigging above the roar of the storm, "My God, my God, make haste, make haste" ' (*FL*, 443).

Stanza 20
coifèd (line 2): refers to the head-dress of the order.
double a desperate name (line 3): because name of the country that expelled nuns and name, also, of the ill-fated ship.
two of a town (line 5): Eisleben, also in Germany. Birthplace of St Gertrude, Benedictine nun and mystic, also of Martin Luther a leading figure of the Reformation, therefore, to ultramontane Catholic Hopkins, a 'beast of the waste wood'. He is reflecting on the inextricable mixture of good and evil in the world.
Abel (line 8): archetypal man of righteousness.
Cain (line 8): archetypal murderer (Gen., iv).

Stanza 21
Gnashed (line 5): stresses the violence of nature in contrast with the remote peace of God above.
Orion (line 5): constellation named after a hunter. Hopkins is referring to God who dwells apart, yet who pursues the destiny of men.
unchancelling (line 6): the chancel is the part of the church where the altar stands. The nuns had been 'unchancelled' by the Falk laws.
poising palms (line 6): i.e. of God's hands, bringing good out of evil, measuring the worth of the nuns' sufferings described above.
line 8: an image of beauty and tranquillity housed in a line meditatively long drawn out. The violent elements of the nuns' sufferings were already transmuted in Heaven into things of joy and beauty.

Stanza 22
The coincidence of there being five nuns and Christ having had five wounds produces a finely wrought meditation on Christ's passion continued in time.

finding (line 1): discovery. To find this pattern of wounds is to find Christ.
sake (line 1): outward stamp which shows forth unique essence of a man.
See note 'sake' in Henry Purcell sonnet (p. 90).
cipher (line 2): symbol or device (as in heraldry).
Mark (line 3): i.e. take notice that, etc.
word (line 4): inner meaning.
lines 5–6: Christ inflicts similar wounds on his chosen and predestined ones, those most dear to him. See Eph., i, 4–7.
Stigma (line 7): a mark that sets the bearer apart from others.
cinquefoil (line 7): five-petalled like a rose window. Refers to the fivefold wounds.
lamb (line 8): the eternal sign of blood-sacrifice.
rose-flake (line 8): i.e. of martydom. Christ's body, both physical and mystical, is eternally marked with the wounds of sacrifice.

Stanza 23
Father Francis (line 1): the nuns were of the order founded by St Francis of Assisi (1182–1226), famed for his holiness and for the stigmata—the five wounds of Christ—he carried on his body.
his (line 3): i.e. Christ's, the Life that died.
Lovescape (line 4): the five wounds are the 'scape' or visible pattern of God's love for men. Francis received Christ's lovescape'—i.e. the five wounds of crucifixion.
seal of his seraph-arrival (line 5): St Francis, bearing the marks of Christ's death, would be assured of following Christ in his resurrection and arrival into heaven.
Nigel Foxell quotes the following lines from the *'Terza Considerazione delle Stimmate'*:
St Francis ... began most devoutly to contemplate the Passion of Christ and His infinite Love: and fervour of devotion so grew in him that everything became transformed into Jesus for love and compassion. Thus remaining, and fired by this contemplation, he saw ... a Seraph coming from heaven with six resplendent flaming wings. This Seraph flew swiftly towards St Francis, so that he could see him and realize that he had in him the image of man crucified.
(*Ten Poems Analysed*, Pergamon Press (Oxford, 1966, p. 246)
To bathe in his fall-gold mercies, etc. (line 8): recalls the God of mercy ('fall-gold') but also of terrible majesty ('all-fire') that Hopkins has been speaking of throughout the poem. The nuns are sealed into Christ's death, not by the five wounds as was their founder-father Francis, but by being 'bathed' in dark waters. (See Rom., vi.) This is their baptism, which is death but

also birth into life eternal. The 'all-fire glances' refers both to the terror of their death, also to seeing God face to face after death. (1 Cor., xiii, 12.) Nigel Foxell also points out that the images of gold and fire derive from Italian pictures of the Stigmata. One picture shows gold lines linking St Francis's wounds with those of Christ, and the '*Terza Considerazione*' speaks of a 'most beautiful and resplendent flame' above the saint's head. (ibid.)

This line is also an almost perfect example of 'traverse' *cynghanedd* where the alliterative pattern of the latter half of the line corresponds to that of the first half.

To bathe in his fall-gold mercies, to breathe in his all-fire glances.
1   2   3   4 5 6 7   1   2   3   5 4   67

In the next stanza, Hopkins's thought turns to Wales where he learned this art and where he was at the time of the disaster.

Stanza 24

christens her wild-worst Best (line 8): recognizes the presence of Christ in the storm.

Stanzas 25–7

In these stanzas Hopkins asks what it was that drove the nun to call out in this way to Christ.

Stanza 25

arch and original breath (line 2): the poet invokes the Holy Spirit.

line 3: 'Does she long to be as her lover [Christ] was—dead and rising to immortality?'

else-minded then (line 5): if so (i.e. if line 3 is true), then the disciples who were afraid of drowning, were not of the same mind. See Matt., viii, 25.

men woke (lines 5–6): i.e. men (who) woke.

crown (line 7): of martyrdom.

the keener, etc. (line 8): more than ever eager to be with Christ since she was feeling the pangs of approaching death.

Stanza 26

For how, etc. (line 1): follows on from previous lines and illustrates the contrast between the blind anguish of death and the bliss that follows. 'For how cheering it is to the heart when the grey [fog or mist] disappears and the beauty of May is revealed.' Hopkins is also referring to the religious life which, though willingly undertaken, was so often arid and bleak for him.

down-dugged, ground-hugged (line 2): downy-breasted billowings of fog, 'hugged' close by the earth.

jay-blue (line 3): blue, the colour of Mary, and of the May sky, Mary's month. Hopkins wrote to Dixon that at one time in his life 'crimson and pure blues seemed to me spiritual and heavenly sights fit to draw tears once' (*D*, 38).

Blue-beating, etc. (line 5): the soft radiance and intensity of these images is conveyed by sound as much as by logical sense.

What by your measure, etc. (line 7): he has given these images of Heaven and he asks the reader directly what is his 'measure' (idea, image) of Heaven.

The treasure, etc. (line 8): that eye hath not seen nor ear heard. See I Cor., ii, 9.

Stanza 27

it was not these (line 1): the poet concludes that it was not the danger of that moment, but rather a lifetime of remembered toil and weariness ('time's tasking') that caused her to call upon her Master to make haste.

The jading and jar, etc. (line 2): a rough paraphrase would be: 'It is the daily grind and unpleasantness of life that "fathers" [causes, begets] the plea for relief from the overburdened heart—not the thought of danger.' Hopkins here is obviously speaking from his own heart.

sodden-with-its-sorrowing heart (line 4): cf. 'Selfyeast of spirit, a dull dough sours' ('I wake and feel' sonnet. See also other of the 'terrible' sonnets.)

electrical horror (line 5): not one of Hopkins's happiest. See 'The Loss of the Eurydice', line 24.

then further it finds (line 5): the heart finds Christ's passion a solace in quiet contemplation, not in the heat of action and danger. Hopkins is giving another reason for rejecting any unduly romantic views of the nun's action.

Other, I gather (line 7): emphasis on the 'I'. He affirms his personal opinion of the nun's motives.

Stanza 28

But how shall I . . . make me room, etc. (line 1): he returns to the scene of the wreck. In these truncated exclamations (aposiopesis) he merges the last cries of the doomed with his own gasping efforts to evoke the scene in words.

Ipse (line 5): (Latin) himself.

Do, deal, lord it (line 7): addressed to Christ directly, *or* could be prefaced with 'He was to . . .', to follow line above.

doom (line 8): will or decision. He asks that Christ should do His will quickly.

Stanza 29

unshapeable shock night (line 3): elliptical phrase. 'unshapeable' in the sense that the human mind could make no sense of its horror. Hopkins may also have had in mind his own 'unshapeable shock night'. See note on 'Thou knowest', st. 2, l. 5.

wording it (line 5): interpreting it.

word of (line 6): expression of, message of.

worded by (line 6): given meaning by.

A paraphrase of lines 1–6 might be: 'There was one heart, one eye, that read correctly the events of that night, interpreting the disaster in the light of Him who created Heaven and earth, and who gives meaning to all things.'

Simon Peter of a soul (line 7): i.e. a rock of a soul, both in the sense of being firm in adversity, but also in the deeper sense of being the kind of sacrificial soul that builds the Church. See Matt., xvi, 18.

Tarpeian-fast, but, etc. (line 8): as immovable as the Tarpeian rock (a cliff outside Rome) yet shedding light on the whole world.

Stanza 30

Lines 1–4 are of Herbertian sweetness and simplicity—calm after storm.

the feast (line 3): in the sense of rejoicing in Heaven, also in the sense that the next day, 8 December, was the Feast of the Immaculate Conception of Mary 'one woman without stain', celebrated by the whole Church on earth.

lines 7–8: in a mystical sense this nun was another Mary who by the quality of her death 'uttered' (showed forth, gave birth to) Christ in the world.

Stanzas 31–5

The poem draws away from immediate contact with its subject and closes with a meditation upon the ways of God.

Stanza 31

Well, she has thee (line 1): she is rewarded for her pain and patience.

but pity of the rest, etc. (line 2): the poet grieves at first that the rest on board have gone to death 'comfortless, unconfessed' but realizes that, by a 'lovely-felicitous Providence', the nun, by her bearing in face of death, has probably brought many to Christ. So shipwreck may be harvest, of souls 'saved' for God.

Stanza 32
Yore-flood (line 2): the Deluge (Gen., vii) or the primal waters of Creation (Gen., i, 2).
The recurb, etc. (line 3): God with His power girds in the oceans of the world which He Himself has created.
Stanching (line 5): checking the flow to waste. God, as giving order to the ever-threatening chaos of man's psychic life, was a constant thought to Hopkins. See st. 4.
past all/Grasp (lines 6–7): compound adjective applied to 'God'.

Stanza 33
outrides/The all of water (lines 1–2): God's mercy is greater than the world's oceans.
Lower than death (line 4): see Rom., viii, 39. Syntax is '[an ark] for the lingerer with a love [that] glides lower', etc.
A vein for the visiting (line 5): Christ is a medium through whom prayer can be directed for those who, themselves, are past prayer, the souls in Purgatory.
the uttermost mark . . . fetched (lines 6–8): Christ in His death, plunged to these depths and redeemed them, before triumphing over them in His Resurrection. See Eph., iv, 9–10.

Stanza 34
new born (line 1): because newly manifested to the world in the nun's death. See st. 30, l. 8.
Double-naturèd (line 2): 'True God and true Man.'
maiden-furled (line 3): enclosed in the womb of Mary.
Mid-numbered He (line 5): Christ is the second of the three 'persons' (translated by one theologian as 'modes of being') of the Godhead— 'three of the thunder-throne'.
Not a dooms-day dazzle, etc. (line 6): not in the terror of the Last Judgment, nor in the obscurity of the Incarnation 'as he came'.
lines 7–8: Hopkins reaffirms that this disaster has been a brief and local visit by God who, although 'kind', has firmly called his own ones to Him. The disaster has been one of His dark mercies. See st. 12.
let flash to the shire (line 8): appearing only within a limited area.

Stanza 35
Dame, at our door, etc. (line 1): a prayer to the soul of the dead nun to pray for those who labour to bring Christ back to England.

easter (line 5): used as a verb, meaning 'rise'. As frequently happens, there is a double association of the sun rising in the east and Christ rising at Easter to new life.

rare-dear Britain (line 6): despite his despair at our godless industrial civilization (e.g. 'The Sea and the Skylark') Hopkins was intensely patriotic.

Our hearts', etc. (line 8): an ecstatic crescendo of genitives. Christ is the fire of charity in the hearts of men, the Lord of all our noblest aims and thoughts.

Note to the reader

Now that you have worked through the poem and captured the main drift of Hopkins's logical meaning, it is suggested that you read the poem again without notes. More than most poems this ode or elegy is a 'shape which is contemplated for its own sake' over and above the logical meaning. Read it again for its verbal excitement, the multiple associations of some of its words and phrases, and the ecstatic lift and roll of its rhythms.

The Silver Jubilee
(*St Beuno's, 1876*)

This is a public poem written for a special occasion. Writing in April 1879 to Bridges, Hopkins said, 'It seems to me to hit the mark it aims at without any wrying.' He admitted in the same letter that he felt himself to 'come short' in his 'popular pieces'—i.e. this poem and the 'May Magnificat' (*B*, 77–8).

The occasion was the Silver Jubilee of Dr James Brown, 1812–81, first Roman Catholic Bishop of Shrewsbury, a diocese which at first included Shropshire, Chester and the six counties of North Wales. Hopkins, writing to his father, described the celebrations at St Beuno's as follows:

. . . *on Sunday we presented him with an album containing a prose address and compositions, chiefly verse, in many languages, among which were Chinese and Manchoo, all by our people, those who had been or were to be ordained by his lordship. The Chinese and Manchoo . . . were by a little German, very very learned, with a beaky nose like a bugle horn, and they were beautifully penned by himself. For the Welsh they had to come to me, for, sad to say, no one else in the house knows anything about it; I also wrote in Latin and English, and the English was the aforesaid Silver Jubilee. Fr Morris preached first, for the presentation took place in Church, and after Mass the Bishop sat on a throne and received the address and album and a cheque for £100 with it. In the afternoon was a high dinner and music at dessert and the Silver Jubilee was set effectively by a very musical and very noisy member of the community and was sung as a glee by the choir.*
(*FL*, 140)

The Welsh and Latin poems, also by Hopkins, can be found in the third edition of his poems numbers 135 and 136 and in the fourth edition numbers 172 and 173. The English version was published in the Jesuit magazine *The Month*, the editors of which, however, were subsequently to refuse both 'The Wreck of the Deutschland' and 'The Loss of the Eurydice'.

Stanza 1
no high-hung bells (line 1): Roman Catholic churches at the time were forbidden to ring bells.

Stanza 2
Five and twenty years, etc. (line 1): In the 1850 the Roman Catholic hierarchy was restored to England and Wales, 'sacred fountains . . . that but now were shut'.

Stanza 3

this her true . . . Silver Jubilee (lines 3–4): because the authentic twenty-fifth year of the first episcopate of Shrewsbury diocese. Actually it was, as Hopkins himself remarked, the twenty-sixth year, but the Jubilee would still be true because commemorating the refounding of the 'true Church'.

Stanza 4

some way spent (line 2): Bishop Brown was sixty-four. He was to retire three years later, broken in health by his prolonged labours for the diocese, which he greatly developed during his episcopate.

Metre: the rhythm of the poem suggests both a triumphal Horatian ode and an English carol with refrain. It would sound well 'sung as a glee' as Hopkins describes.

Penmaen Pool
(August 1876)

It was the custom for the students studying Theology at St Beuno's to spend some portion of the summer months at a house at Barmouth owned by the Jesuit Order. While on holiday here the students would take advantage of the tide on the Mawddach estuary and row up the river to Penmaen Pool, where they would lunch at the George Inn. This poem was written for the Visitors' Book at the inn. Several copies of the MS 'exist and vary' according to Bridges. The custom of 'George Day' during summer holidays at Barmouth still continues among the theological students.

This version is from a MS dated from 'Barmouth, Merionethshire'.

tackle and tool (line 6): a form of words developed later in 'Pied Beauty'; 'And all trades their gear and tackle and trim'.
Cadair cliff (line 7): Cader Idris (2,927 ft.) lies south of the Mawddach.
Dyphwys dim (line 9): Diffwys (2,624 ft.) three miles north of the Mawddach.
Giant's stool (line 10): ' "Cadair Idris" is written as a note to "Giant's Stool" ' (Bridges).
To halve the bowl (line 12): Hopkins probably means that these two great mountains cast their shadows, from either side, on to the pool.
nature's rule (line 14): originally 'renewal'. Hopkins's father must have protested against rhyming 'renewal' with 'pool' because we find the poet writing to his mother than 'it must be looked at partly as a freak, partly as a necessity' (*FL*, 141). At all events he must have decided to change it.
Charles's Wain (line 17): otherwise known as The Plough, seven stars in the constellation of the Great Bear.
sheep-flock clouds like worlds of wool (line 18): cloudscapes fascinated Hopkins, as can be seen from some very frequent entries in his Journal, as well as such poems as 'Hurrahing in Harvest'—e.g. from 14 May 1867: *... at six in the evening, a wonderful rack of what I hear they call 'flock-of-sheep' clouds, a dapple of plump rounds half parted, half branching from one another like madrepores.*
(*J.* 150. *Madrepores = corals.*)
The Mawddach, how she trips! (line 21)): the Mawddach is an estuary with strong tides, presenting a severe challenge to the oarsman.

Metre: a light-hearted, but skilfully constructed poem in a slightly rollicking iambic tetrameter redolent of Belloc. Nine different rhymes for 'pool', and a number of two-syllabled rhymes add to the racy effect.

God's Grandeur
(February–March 1877)

Hopkins sent two slightly differing versions of this sonnet to Bridges, dated 23 February, and March 1877.

It contrasts the devitalizing and smearing effect produced by man on the face of the earth, with the ever-springing freshness of the life of nature. It was a theme frequently dwelt on by Hopkins in letters and sermons, as well as in such poems as 'The Sea and the Skylark' and 'Ribblesdale'.

charged (line 1): i.e. as a battery is charged. Hopkins used 'electrical' imagery in other poems, e.g. 'The Wreck of the Deutschland', st. 27, 'The Loss of the Eurydice', st. 6.

God's presence, to him, was both beautiful and dangerous like lightning. In a meditation of 1881, he wrote:

All things therefore are charged with love, are charged with God and if we know how to touch them give off sparks and take fire, yield drops and flow, ring and tell of him.

(*S*, 195)

like shining from shook foil (line 2): one version had 'lightning' in place of 'shining'. Hopkins wrote to Bridges of the central importance of this image in the poem, and corrected what must have been some misunderstanding:

... I mean foil in its sense of leaf or tinsel, and no other word whatever will give the effect I want. Shaken goldfoil gives off broad glares like sheet lightning and also, and this is true of nothing else, owing to its zigzag dints and creasings and network of small many cornered facets, a sort of fork lightning too.

(*B*, 169)

like the ooze of oil/Crushed (lines 3–4): i.e. like the ooze of oil from crushed olives. Hopkins used the same image in an early poem, 'A Soliloquy of One of the Spies left in the Wilderness':

Who tread the grapes are splayed with stripes of gore,
    And they who crush the oil
Are spatter'd.

Olive oil in Old Testament times was a symbol of power and kingship as well of priesthood. There are also hidden overtones of the fruitful but painful crushing of human self-will under religious discipline, for the greater glory of God.

reck his rod (line 4): care about his (God's) wrath. It grieved Hopkins to see average humanity so heedless of God's law and of the prospect of the hereafter. Later, while at Liverpool, he wrote to Bridges:

And the drunkards go on drinking, the filthy, as the scripture says, are filthy still; human nature is so inveterate. Would I have seen the last of it.
(*B*, 110)

seared with trade: bleared, smeared with toil (line 7): Hopkins wrote this amid the rural peace and beauty of St Beuno's, but it was amply confirmed by his subsequent experience in industrial parishes. He wrote in 1879,

I was yesterday at St Helens, probably the most repulsive place in Lancashire or out of the Black Country. The stench of sulphuretted hydrogen rolls in the air and fills of the same gas form on railing and pavement.
(*B*, 90)

dearest freshness deep down things (line 10): the ever-burgeoning life-processes which constantly renew the face of nature. Hopkins developed this experience in the poem 'Spring'. To him, the freshness of nature was a symbol of psychological and spiritual renewal which he so often needed, and so seldom received. See final line of sonnet 'Thou art indeed just'.

springs (line 12): the word carries overtones of the natural joy of spring, but also of Zacharias's hymn of spiritual joy, at the coming advent of Christ 'the *dayspring* from on high', who comes 'to give light to them that sit in darkness and in the shadow of death, to guide our feet into the way of peace' (Luke, i, 78). In lines 11–14 Hopkins points to the real source of the ever-renewed life of nature—the Holy Ghost which is the creative energy and love of God.

bent | World (lines 13–14): 'bent' in sleep and forgetfulness, while a great spiritual power 'broods' above it as it did at the time of the Creation.

warm breast and with ah! bright wings (line 14): Hopkins is thinking of the Biblical image of the Holy Ghost in the form of a dove. Bridges called this line, with its ecstatic, adoring 'ah', a 'perversion of human feeling' and an example of Hopkins's attempts 'to force emotion into theological or sectarian channels' (Preface to Notes, first edition). Some would agree with this verdict, but many, including W. H. Gardner, would sharply rebut it. There is a carefully wrought rhetorical splendour in the line, effected by a patterning of vowel and consonant sequences, that seems to put it above charges of emotionalism. 'The chiming of consonants I got in part from the Welsh which is very rich in sound and imagery,' wrote Hopkins (*B*, 38).

Metre: a sonnet consisting of octave (8 lines) and sestet (6 lines) with the usual 'volta' or turn of thought after the octave. The rhythm is 'standard rhythm counterpointed'. The standard rhythm of a sonnet is iambic pentameter (5 iambic feet per line) but here this basic rhythm is 'never heard but only counted' (*B*, 46) and the *actual* or heard rhythm is mounted on top of it. Thus the heard and the unheard rhythms run in combination, producing an effect known in music as counterpoint. Milton was the great master of counterpoint in verse and Hopkins is here setting out to try similar experiments (see *B*, 38).

The Starlight Night
(St Beuno's, 24 February 1877)

Another piece written during Hopkins's time at St Beuno's when his vision of God and nature flowered with such intensity. The Sonnet 'God's Grandeur' spoke of a universe charged with energy and beauty, showing forth, though also hiding, the face of God. In this sonnet, which is a particular illustration of this theme the poet looks at the stars, whose purity and radiance were a symbol to him of his own mystical and moral yearnings. 'As we drove home', he wrote in 1874, 'the stars came out thick: I leant back to look at them and my heart opening more than usual praised our Lord to and in whom all that beauty comes home' (*J*, 254).

In the poem he sees the stars as an enchanting world of cities, people, lawns, woods and orchards. In the end, however, all this beauty is only an outward sign of an inner and spiritual Beauty; in Hopkins's own words a 'barn' which houses the Heaven of Christ and his saints.

The bright boroughs, the circle-citadels (line 3): cf. Henry Vaughan the seventeenth-century mystical poet:
They are that city's shining spires
We travel to.
cf. also an early entry (1868) in Hopkins's Journal on the majesty of the stars:
Before sunrise looking out of a window saw a noble scape of stars—the Plough all golden falling, Cassiopeia on end with her bright quains pointing to the right, the graceful bends of Perneus underneath her, and some great star whether Capella or not I am not sure risen over the brow of the mountain. (*J*, 170)
Down in the dim woods the diamond delves (line 4): the darker recesses of the sky which glint mysteriously with points of light, here imagined as the eyes of elves or the flash of diamonds in hidden 'delves' (obs. noun meaning mine or pit). Cf. first draft sent to his mother 'Look the elf-rings! Look at the out-round earnest eyes' (*FL*, 145).
The grey lawns cold, etc. (line 5): the sky at dawnlight with stars still showing. Cf. entry in Journal: 'the skies were then clear and ashy and fresh with stars' (*J*, 201). Hopkins had also written of the 'odd white-gold look of short grass in tufts' (*J*, 150) which explains the association of gold-stars-lawn. The line, however, has a magical quality which eludes any one-to-one source-explanations. Cf. first draft sent to his mother: 'The grey lawns cold where quaking gold dew lies' (*FL*, 145).

Whitebeam ... abeles (line 6): continues the analogy of star-world with nature-world. The whitebeam and abele (white poplar) have leaves with silvery undersides which glint as the wind flutters them.

Flake-doves (line 7): a daring but quite clear expression of white feathers in a farmyard flurry.

all a purchase, etc. (line 8): this last line of the octave turns towards the thought of the sestet that all this created beauty and radiance are symbols of the beauty of Heaven which humanity can 'purchase' by the prayers and good works of the Christian life.

Buy then! bid then (line 9): with the thought of 'purchase' in his mind he continues in the style of an auctioneer, showing the beauty of his wares, and urging his hearers to pay the simple price of 'Prayer, patience, alms, vows'.

Look look: a May-mess (line 10): i.e. the richly-massed stars like May blossom on fruit trees. The latter, at the time, had a visionary quality for Hopkins which gave him intense joy—see 'The May Magnificat', p. 83–5.

mealed-with-yellow sallows (line 11): 'Sallow' is the pussy willow. 'Mealed-with-yellow' because of the soft furry quality of the yellow flowers.

These are indeed the barn (line 12): these created beauties are only the outer covering. Father Devlin, commenting on Hopkins's sermons and spiritual writings, points out that after reading Scotus (q.v.), Hopkins saw the world as having been created expressly for the redemptive work of Christ: 'The worlds of angels and of men were created as fields for Christ, in which to exercise his adoration of the Father, fields for him to sow and work and harvest. Hence, perhaps, the imagery of grain and barn that ran through Hopkins's poetry, 1876–8' (*S*, 109).

This piece-bright paling (line 13): in first draft 'pale and parclose': the canopy of stars, here imagined as a fence studded with light hiding the true Heaven where dwell Christ, his Mother Mary (assumed bodily into Heaven according to the dogma of the Assumption) and all the saints. The line has the literal quaintness and mystical intensity of an early Italian painting—W. H. Gardner suggests Mantegna. The medieval word 'hallows' (i.e. saints, cf. All-hallows = all saints) adds to this effect.

shocks (line 14): stooks, or sheaves of wheat. The whole context suggests the passage in Matt., xiii, of the good wheat of humanity gathered into the 'barn' of Heaven.

Metre: Standard sonnet rhythm, but 'opened', i.e. both octave and sestet are in sprung rhythm; also counterpointed, i.e. built upon a basic rhythmic pattern but departing from it without annulling it. See metre note to 'God's Grandeur'.

Spring
(St Beuno's, May 1877)

A sonnet which contemplates the loveliness of spring and points it back to its original source—Paradise—the Garden of Eden and the innocence of mankind before the Fall.

weeds, in wheels (line 2): the expression is there mainly for the carolling effect of the sound. However, W. H. Gardner suggests: 'Prominent among the weeds that "shoot in wheels" are the blackberry stems, the regular arcs of which are so characteristic of English commons and hedgerows' (*WHG*, Vol. II, 238). The thought may have originated in an early Journal entry of 15 May 1866:
To see the long forward-creeping curls of the newly-leaved trees, in sweeps and rows all lodged one with another down the meadow edge, beautiful . . .
(*J*, 136)
look little low heavens (line 3): lit. 'look like etc.', but the expression conveys some numinous quality 'looking' out from within the eggs. Writing to Dixon three years later from the grime of industrial Liverpool, Hopkins wrote:
I remember that crimson and pure blues seemed to me spiritual and heavenly sights fit to draw tears once; now I can just see what I once saw, but can hardly dwell on it and should not care to do so.
(*D*, 38)
rinse and wring (line 4): words whose sound and meaning convey the ecstatic intensity of the experience (cf. 'weeds, in wheels'). 'Rinse' has overtones of the Asperges—the sprinkling of purifying Holy Water. 'Wring' suggests both bell-like clarity and purity of sound and the over-whelming, echoing invasion of the ear.
glassy (line 6): an adjective evoking the jewelled radiant quality that accompanies such visionary writing on Paradise; cf. Milton, *Paradise Lost*, Book IV, 146–50, 246–50; Rev., xxi and xxii.
What is all this juice, etc. (line 9): in the sestet, Hopkins asks and answers the question of the source of the joyful fecundity of springtime. It is a 'strain' (echo, reminder or symbol) of the loveliness of earth in the beginning.
Have, get, etc. (line 11): the general sense is an urgent plea to Christ to claim for himself the minds of young people before they become 'sour with sinning'. Hopkins wrote later of youth:

This, all this beauty blooming,
This, all this freshness fuming,
Give God while worth consuming.
('Morning Midday and Evening Sacrifice')

sour with sinning (line 12): Hopkins was to write in 1880, 'And the drunkards go on drinking, the filthy, as the Scripture says, are filthy still: human nature is so inveterate' (*B*, 110).

Most . . . thy choice (line 14): because the gift of oneself to Christ when in prime of youth is of great value. In an 1879 sermon, Hopkins was to say: *. . . which leads me to say, brethren, by the way, the man or woman, the boy or girl, that in their bloom and heyday, in their strength and health give themselves to God and with fresh body and joyously beating blood give him glory, how near he will be to them in age and sickness and wall their weakness round in the hour of death.* (*S*, 19)

O maid's child (line 14): i.e. Christ himself, son of Mary.

Metre: Standard rhythm, opening with sprung leadings. Line 1 is deliberately sprung, abrupt and irregular.

In the Valley of the Elwy
(*1877*)

This sonnet is a priestly meditation on fallen mankind, and here, as in 'Ribblesdale' and elsewhere, the contrast is between the loveliness of nature and the unloveliness of man. It is *not* a specific attack on the Welsh.

Bridges must have misunderstood the poem, so Hopkins had to explain: *The frame of the sonnet is a rule of three sum* wrong, *thus: As the sweet smell to those kind people so the Welsh landscape is NOT to the Welsh; and then the author and principle of all four terms is asked to bring the sum right.*
(*B*, 76)

The argument of the poem is roughly as follows: 'I remember a house where the atmosphere was sweet and comforting. This atmosphere was as protective to these good people as the wing of a bird over her eggs or the mild nights of spring over tender growing things. It seemed natural that this should be so. There is a similar loveliness and peace about the landscape of Wales. But in this case "the inmate does not correspond".' The poem ends with a prayer that God will make good the deficiency here, in the inmate, i.e. mankind in general.

The poem is notable mainly for its limpid sweetness of diction and for the evocation of household peace in the first few lines, probably a pleasant memory in Hopkins's somewhat comfortless and institutionalized life.

I remember a house (line 1): Hopkins revealed to Bridges: 'The kind of people of the sonnet were the Watsons of Shooter's Hill, nothing to do with the Elwy' (*B*, 76).

That cordial air (line 5): this is a Welsh (not a Shooter's Hill) memory.

made those kind people a hood (line 5): i.e. made a hood (for) those kind people.

Why, it seemed of course (line 8): the question of *why* the air should be so kind to these people never occurred, as it seemed natural that it should be.

combes (line 9): valleys, or rather the gentle dips between hills.

All the air things wear, etc. (line 10): i.e. '[and lovely also is] the very look and feel of things that make up Wales'.

Only the inmate does not correspond (line 11): see notes on the final lines of 'The Sea and the Skylark', p. 65.

swaying considerate scales (line 12): cf. the 'poising palms' of God the merciful judge in 'The Wreck of the Deutschland', st. 21.

Complete thy creature (line 13): a prayer that God will make good the deficiencies of man.

Metre: a sonnet in standard rhythm, but also 'sprung and counterpointed'. Normally, sprung rhythm, with its freedom in respect of number of syllables, excludes counterpoint which is a variant on standard rhythm with its basic ten syllables per line. Here he mingles the two systems, 'the most delicate and difficult business of all', as he remarked to Bridges (*B*, 45).

In the MS into which Bridges copied many of Hopkins's poems as they came to hand, and in which Hopkins from time to time made amendments, 11. 4 and 9 are marked as follows:

1.4 '*I remember a house* ...

1.9 '... *waters, meadows* ...

In this case the mark means that one stress is spread over two syllables.

The Sea and the Skylark
(Rhyl, May 1877)

This sonnet, which has the same tight economy of rhyme as 'God's Grandeur', was first called 'Walking by the Sea'. It is notable for the onomatopoeic effects of the first two quatrains, produced by a skilful patterning of vowel and consonant—slow and ponderous in the first, suggesting the eternal sea, and swift and wild in the second, suggesting the pure spirited ecstasy of the skylark.

So much attention is paid to the arrangement of vowel and consonant—the 'lettering' to use Hopkins's term—that he must have thought he had sacrificed some of the sense in the process. He wrote to Bridges five years later: *It was written in my Welsh days, in my salad days when I was fascinated with* cynghanedd *or consonant chime, and, as in Welsh* englyns, *the 'sense' as one of themselves said, 'gets the worst of it'.*
(*B*, 163)
He added, with some truth, that the difficulty was 'far from glaring'.

The theme is a familiar one with Hopkins: the lifegiving purity of nature and the sordidness of the civilization that man is creating. It is certainly not an attack on Rhyl nor indeed on the Welsh. Indeed, Hopkins wrote to his mother in 1874, 'I have always looked upon myself as half Welsh and so I warm to them' (*FL*, 127). Like 'Ribblesdale' and others, this poem is simply a general meditation on nature and man, occasioned by a given scene.

On ear and ear (line 1): far more penetrating than 'on either ear'.
Trench (line 2): a verb, suggesting vivid impact.
ramps (line 2): once again a word rich in sound-association, romp, rampage, ram.
lull-off or all roar (line 3): for a similar description of tidal water compare Matthew Arnold's 'Dover Beach'.
Left hand, off land, etc. (line 5): an example of vowelling-off up a scale to the word 'ascend'.
His rash-fresh rewinded new-skeinèd score (line 6): in the original version of this much recast poem, the lines read (more clearly):
Left hand, off land, I hear the lark ascend,
With rash-fresh more, repair of skein and score,
Race wild reel round, crisp coil deal down to floor,
And spill music till there's none left to spend.
(printed, *B*, 163, footnote)

Hopkins was obliged to send an enormously detailed explanation of this quatrain to Bridges. The relevant portions are as follows—the words in roman are those which appear in some form or other in the poem itself. The explanation pertains to the earlier version, but obviously applies also to the final one:

'Rash-fresh *more*' *(it is dreadful to explain these things in cold blood) means a headlong and exciting new snatch of singing, resumption by the lark of his song, which by turns he gives over and takes up again all day long, and this goes on, the sonnet says,*[1] *through all time.*
(*B*, 164)

The skein *and* coil *are the lark's song, which from his height gives the impression (not to me only) of something falling to the earth and not vertically quite but tricklingly or wavingly, something as* a skein of silk ribbed *by having been tightly wound on a narrow card . . . or as fishing tackle or twine* unwinding from a reel or winch . . .
(ibid.)

The same is called a score in the musical sense of score *and this score is* 'writ upon a liquid sky *trembling to welcome it*', *only not horizontally.*
(ibid.)

He concluded this laborious explanation as follows:
The lark in wild glee *races the reel round, paying or dealing out and down the turns of the skein or coil right to the earth floor, the ground, where it lies in a heap, as it were, or rather is all wound off on to another winch, reel, bobbin, or spool in Fancy's eye by the moment the bird touches earth and so is ready for a fresh unwinding at the next flight.*
(ibid.)

Finally, perhaps aware of the pedestrian and turgid quality of the foregoing, he added,
There is, you see, plenty meant; but the saying of it smells, I fear of the lamp, of salad oil, and, what is nastier, in one line somewhat of Robert Browning.
(ibid.)

crisps (line 7): '"Crisps" means almost "crisped", namely with notes' (ibid.)
ring right out (line 10): i.e. expose by contrast. The sound of the sea and the song of the skylark are pure, elemental and timeless. By contrast, the seaside town looks valueless and ephemeral.
sordid turbid time (line 10): 'turbid' = muddy. After a few years, Hopkins had this opinion more than ever confirmed. He wrote to Dixon in 1881:
My Liverpool and Glasgow experience laid upon my mind a conviction, a truly crushing conviction, of the misery of town life to the poor . . . of the degrada-

---

[1] *i.e.* 'rewinded new-skeined'.

tion even of our race, of the hollowness of this century's civilization: it made even life a burden to me to have daily thrust on me the things I saw.
(*D*, 97)

life's pride and cared-for crown (line 11): because appointed lord of nature, and created 'a little lower than the angels'. Man gives God glory 'even by his being, beyond all visible creatures' (*S*, 239). He gives God *conscious* glory, wrote Hopkins, being 'more highly pitched, selved and distinctive than anything in the world' (Retreat Notes. *S*, 122).

earth's past prime (line 12): the morning of the human race, when, to use Hopkins's paraphrase of Genesis iii, 8, 'God in some sensible form walked in Paradise' (*S*, 165). See also the sonnet 'Spring'.

Our make and making break, etc. (line 13): the syntax is obscure but the meaning is clear enough. It is a comment on the destructiveness of nineteenth-century industrial materialism, smearing the earth with ugliness and degrading untold masses of people. The energy of God which tends always to create beauty is being defeated by man, as if the latter wished to return to primordial slime—a 'challenging inversion of the Darwinian thesis', as W. H. Gardner points out (*WHG*, Vol. II, 248). In a well-known passage under the title of Instructions, Hopkins wrote (or said):

No, we have not answered God's purposes, we have not reached the end of our being. Are we God's orchard or God's vineyard? we have yielded rotten fruit, sour grapes, or none. Are we his cornfield sown? we have not come to ear or are mildewed in the ear. Are we his farm? it is a losing one to him. Are we his tenants? we have refused him rent. Are we his singing bird? we will not learn to sing. Are we his pipe or harp? we are out of tune, we grate upon his ear. Are we his glass to look in? we are deep in dust or our silver gone or we are broken or, worst of all, we misshape his face and make God's image hideous.
(*S*, 240)

See also notes on relevant passages in 'God's Grandeur' and 'Ribblesdale', also note on 'fuming' (line 6) in 'Morning Midday and Evening Sacrifice'.

Metre: standard rhythm, sometimes counterpointed. Some 'sprung' lines, e.g. lines 2, 6, 11.

The Windhover
To Christ Our Lord
(St Beuno's, 30 May 1877)

'The best thing I ever wrote', said Hopkins of this poem. It is also one of the most discussed, partly because of the rich associations of the language, and partly because of the question of the precise relationship of the sestet to the octet.

The subtitle of the poem is important, because it is a clue to 'my chevalier' who is Christ. 'Chevalier' is a term from French medieval chivalry carrying with it associations of royalty, knighthood, heroism, gentleness, beauty and valour. Hopkins, following the Ignatian Spiritual Exercises would often meditate on Christ in precisely these terms. In a fine sermon given in 1879 at Bedford Leigh he said,

But Christ he is the hero. He too is the hero of a book or books of the divine Gospels. He is a warrior and a conqueror . . . He is a king, Jesus of Nazareth king of the Jews . . . He is a statesman, that drew up the new Testament in his blood and founded the Roman Catholic Church that cannot fail. He is a thinker, that taught us divine mysteries. He is an orator and poet, as in his eloquent words and parables appears. He is all the world's hero, the desire of nations . . . He is the truelove and the bridegroom of men's souls; the virgins follow him whithersoever he goes; the martyrs follow him through a sea of blood, through great tribulation; all his servants take up their cross and follow him.
(S, 35)

The general theme is that the 'brute' (i.e. purely natural) beauty of the falcon is only a faint flash of the splendour of Christ, whose power and energy are of another order 'a billion/Times told lovelier, more dangerous'. It is not merely that Hopkins has found an analogy for spiritual beauty in the material world; rather, he is pointing to the hidden and terrible splendour of sacrificial suffering, which breaks forth upon the world only when all is accomplished. Hence the images of buckling, gashing and galling which recall the crucifixion—hence too the images of painful plod and bleak embers which is often the lot of those who follow Christ in a religious order. Beside this beauty of voluntary redemptive sacrifice, the beauty of the natural and created order is nothing; in fact the latter can find no consummation without the former. Not all these ideas are fully articulated in the poem itself, but there is ample evidence that they formed the theological framework in Hopkins's mind, within which the poem was written.

I caught (line 1): more dynamic than 'saw', as it inscapes the moment of the encounter of the royal, free falcon with the humble, duty-bound priest-poet. A number of entries in his Journal relate to hawks, one of them recording 'a hawk also was hanging on the hover' (*J*, 252).

minion (line 1): darling. The falcon, glamorous and free, is the 'dauphin', the crown prince or royal heir, to the whole world of daylight. W. H. Gardner notes that the Dauphin in Shakespeare's *Henry V* calls his horse, Le cheval volant, *the Pegasus,* qui a les narines de feu. *When I bestride him I soar, I am a hawk: he trots the air.* (Act III, scene vii. Quoted in Notes to Penguin edition, p. 227)

This thought and language is closely echoed by Hopkins, even to the appearance of the word 'dauphin'.

dapple-dawn-drawn (line 2): i.e. attracted from his lair by the dappled dawn.

rolling level underneath him (line 3): a compound adjective which qualifies 'air'. 'Steady' is either another adjective qualifying 'air' or else an additional adverb qualifying 'level', which modifies 'rolling'.

rung upon the rein (line 4): he 'reins' himself in, momentarily hovering. To 'ring upon the rein' is a metaphor from horse-training, meaning to check on the end of a very long rein. Critics have also pointed out the rein/reign overtone, of majesty.

wimpling (line 4): fluttering or rippling.

Then off, off forth (line 5): the rhythm of the words suggest the surging swooping flight.

bow-bend (line 6): a wide arc.

Rebuffed (line 7): mastered. The gusty onomatopoeia is obvious.

Achieve (line 8): achievement, perfection.

My heart in hiding (line 8): i.e. humble and obscure in contrast to the bird. In the sestet, the contemplation of the bird is transformed dramatically into something far greater; the poet's heart stirs and then comes the flash-point of revelation.

Buckle (line 10): a much discussed key word, which can be taken either as imperative or indicative in mood. The following senses can be picked out, each supplementary to one another:

1. 'Buckle' in the sense of a sudden snapping together or fusing of all the merely natural or 'brute' perfections of the bird into an ecstatic moment of recognition by the poet that the whole inscape is charged with the presence of God. In this moment, the supernatural breaks through, and all is glory, similar to the moment described in 'Hurrahing in Harvest'. Nature alone, said Hopkins, is without consciousness, and can only give 'dull glory'; only in man and through the mind and soul of man can she give God full glory.

2. 'Buckle' in the sense of the bending and breaking of the natural order. Nothing literally happens to the falcon, but its beauty and pride metaphorically buckle into insignificance in the power of the revelation it brings with it. Hopkins would associate this with the divine splendour of Christ, which was shed upon the world only when his physical beauty was quite literally wrecked in his total self sacrifice:

... in his bearing how majestic, how strong and yet how lovely and lissom in his limbs, in his look how earnest, grave but kind. In his Passion all this strength was spent, this lissomness crippled, this beauty wrecked, this majesty beaten down.

(*S*, 36)

3. 'Buckle' in the sense of the natural order 'bending the knee' to a supernatural and transcendent beauty.

AND (line 10): the capitals express the dramatic moment of revelation. Hopkins was studying Welsh at the time and, as Father Devlin points out, 'the Welsh *a*, meaning "and" can have the force of an affirmative copula' (*S*, 293).

fire (line 10): the world, to Hopkins, was 'charged' with the grandeur of God, which is ready to 'flame out'[1] whenever the right beholder is there.[2] In the sudden revelation of God's majesty in the sight of the falcon, the divine fire or energy breaks into the world.

more dangerous (line 11): because the love of God can be terrible and consuming. (See 'The Wreck of the Deutschland' st. 2–3.)

O my chevalier (line 11): addressed *through* the falcon *to* Christ, who created the bird and sustains it in being, and of whom the splendour of the bird is a living symbol.

No wonder of it (line 12): much discussed. The 'billion Times told lovelier' fire has broken forth in the encounter between the priest/poet and the falcon. No wonder, because the heart of a servant of God has been purified by the 'plod' of religious obedience and will 'shine" and instantly reflect God's glory whenever it meets it. Though apparently cold like 'blue-bleak embers', it will flame with the fire of love when 'galled' (jarred and rubbed open) and 'gashed' in some crisis—in this case the priest's encounter with the bird. The notion of purification through the frequently grinding routine of the religious life is mentioned in several places by Hopkins, and in the poem 'Morning Midday and Evening Sacrifice' he was again to use the image of a glowing core of heat under embers to describe the life given to the love of God. In one of his most eloquent passages in the sermon quoted above, he spoke of the poverty and laboriousness of Christ's life, which must be lived also by his followers:

[1] *'God's Grandeur'.*   [2] *See 'Hurrahing in Harvest'.*

Poor was his station, laborious his life, bitter his ending: through poverty, through labour, through crucifixion his majesty of nature more shines.
(*S*, 37)

ah my dear (line 13): because the blue-bleak embers recall Christ's dying body. George Herbert, thinking of Christ crucified, wrote: 'Ah my dear, I cannot look on thee.'

gash gold-vermilion (line 14): royal heraldic colours. Also vermilion, the colour of the royal blood from the gash in Christ's side, the 'gold' that redeemed the world.

Metre: a sonnet in sprung rhythm. Five stresses per line, but with extra-metrical or 'outriding' feet, marked by Hopkins in the manuscript with nether loops, e.g.

```
  x  x  /  x    //  x  x  x  //   x   //  x  x  x  / x
dom of daylight's dauphin, dapple-dawn-drawn Falcon in his riding

  x  x  // x  x x  / x  //   x   x x x  /  x   /  x
Of the rolling level underneath him steady air, and striding.
```

Outriding feet are 'thrown away' in the reading.

Pied Beauty
(*St Beuno's, Summer 1877*)

In this Curtal Sonnet (see below, 'Metre') the poet gives glory to God for the rich colour-dappling of the world of nature. In lines 8–11 he praises the Father of all this ever-changing variety and contrast, whose own beauty is eternal, therefore 'past change'. This is a 'Scotist' poem in the sense that Hopkins, following Scotus, is preoccupied with the intense particularity and distinctiveness of natural things. It has the same visionary quality seen in 'As kingfishers catch fire', though the underlying philosophy is not as highly articulated as in the later poem.

skies of couple-colour (line 2): Hopkins's Journal is full of minute descriptions of skyscapes, e.g.
Last Friday fortnight we were out above the Hinkseys on a charming day, sky pied with clouds, near the earthline egg-blue, the longest graceful waved ribbons, also two columns of detached stacked clouds filing far away.
(*J*, 135)
brinded (line 2): i.e. brindled, an archaic word meaning streaked or two-coloured.
Fresh fire-coal, chestnut-falls (line 4): Hopkins noted in his Journal: 'Chestnuts as bright as coals or spots of vermilion'. This vision of Nature glowing from within with Paradisal colour and life is characteristic of Hopkins in the time of his spiritual formation. This, for example, from the Journal in 1873:
We passed the beautiful little mill Hamlet of Balaglas in the glen and started a shining flight of doves to settle on the roof. There is a green rich thickleaved alder by the bridge, and ashes and rocks maroon-red below water up the glen ... The rock is limestone, smooth and pale white ... stained red where the water runs and smoothly and vertically hewed by the force of the brook into highwalled channels with deep pools. The water is so clear in the still pools it is like shadowy air, and in the falls the white is not foamed and chalky, as at Stonyhurst, but like the white of ice or glass.
(*J*, 235)
fold, fallow, and plough (line 5): i.e. grazing fields, fallow land and fields under cultivation, giving the landscape its 'potted and pieced' look.
All things counter (line 7): Hopkins turns from the subject of colour contrast to deeper forms of contrast running in infinite variety throughout nature.
spare (line 7): unique or singular.

whose beauty is past change (line 10): God in Aristotelian philosophy is the Mover of all things, himself unmoved, the Fount of all creation Himself uncreated. Cf. Augustine who spoke of God as 'most ancient Beauty ever-old and ever-new' (*Confessions*).

Metre: This is a Curtal Sonnet, as also is 'Peace'. Hopkins explained that this is an experimental form of sonnet 'constructed in proportions resembling those of the sonnet proper, namely, 6 + 4 instead of 8 + 6, with however a halfline tailpiece'. He described the metre as 'sprung paeonic', a paeonic foot being one stressed plus three unstressed syllables ($/\times\times\times$). As W. H. Gardner points out, however, if each line has five stresses (as it should), then there are only two paeonic feet in the poem, 'colour as a' and 'stipple upon' (*WHG*, Vol. II, 250).

Hurrahing in Harvest
(*September 1877*)

'The Hurrahing sonnet was the outcome of half an hour of extreme enthusiasm as I walked home alone one day from fishing in the Elwy.'

The theme of the poem is an experience of union with Christ as He is alive and present in nature. The idea of Nature as an outward and visible expression of the presence of Christ is found in Hebrews, where Christ is described as:

a Son, who is the radiance of his Father's splendour and the full expression of his being; all creation depends for its support on his enabling word.
(Heb., i, Knox translation)

In the radiance and energy of a windswept autumn day, Hopkins meets his God—not the god of the manuals but a God of fire, energy and beauty suffusing all created forms.

barbarous (line 1): a dissonant word suggesting pagan splendour and energy. The 'stooks' (sheaves of cut wheat or barley, tied with string and stacked upright together to dry) are also 'barbed' and bearded.

wind-walks (line 2): he sees the sky as a celestial highway with the driven clouds 'melting' along it. He had once seen 'a long slender straight river of dull white cloud rolling down all the bed of the Clwyd from as far as I could look up the valley to the sea' (*J*, 260).

lines 3–4: the words, like the clouds, seem to drift along, 'moulding and melting' into one another. Hopkins's Journal is full of carefully observed cloudscapes: 'The bright woolpacks that pelt before a gale in a clear sky are in the tuft and you can see the wind unravelling and rending them finer than any sponge' (*J*, 204). He had also noted some clouds as 'meal-white' (*J*, 204). His poetry often echoes and modifies imagery of his Journal.

glean (line 6): continues the harvest theme. He seeks God in the cloud-scape, and finds Him in mystical encounter.

azurous hung hills (line 9): Hopkins wrote in his Journal: 'The nearer hills, the other side of the valley, showed a hard and *beautifully detached* and glimmering brim against the light . . . *A blue bloom, a sort of meal,* seemed to have spread upon the distant south, enclosed by a basin of hills. Looking all around, but most in looking far up the valley, I felt an instress and charm of Wales' (*J*, 258, September 1874 [Editor's italics]).

as a stallion stalwart (line 10): the poet's feeling of the 'strength' of the hills is conveyed through the alliterated *sound*, rather than through the *visual meaning* of the image, which might in fact distract the reader. This, and the contrasting simile 'very-violet-sweet' have been criticized as 'traps for the attention, not aids for visualization'. This is probably true, but is not a criticism, as sound, not image, is Hopkins's primary mode of conveying meaning.

but the beholder/Wanting (lines 11–12): i.e. lacking. Same idea as in 'The Windhover' of the glory that is born when a human heart, rightly disposed towards God, encounters some splendour in Nature. The poet, looking in and through Nature for the presence of Christ, meets him in a transforming ecstasy. The sense of self and world being hurled upwards by a vast power of love has been experienced both before and since Hopkins; e.g.

And now—there is much more. Instead of myself and my Christ and my love and my prayer, there is the might of a prayer stronger than thunder and milder than the flight of doves rising up from the Priest who is the Centre of the soul of every priest, shaking the foundations of the universe and lifting up—me, Host altar, sanctuary, people, church, abbey, forest, cities, continents, seas, and worlds to God and plunging everything into Him.

(Thomas Merton, *Sign of Jonas*, Hollis & Carter [London, 1953], p. 185)

Metre: This and the other three sonnets of 1877 are the first to use 'outriding' feet. Outriders are:

One, two or three slack syllables added to a foot and not counted in the nominal scanning. They are so called because they seem to hang below the line or ride forward or backward from it in another dimension than the line itself.

(Hopkins's Preface)

For further information, see Introduction, p. 20.

The obvious outriders here are: 'barbarous', 'wind-walks', 'rapturous', 'azurous', 'stalwart', 'hurls for him', 'earth for him'.

Hopkins conceived, but never executed, a new style of music 'something standing to ordinary music as sprung rhythm to common rhythm; it employs quarter tones'. He proposed to set this sonnet to such music.

The Caged Skylark
(*St Beuno's, 1877*)

The theme of the spirit being a prisoner in the body was a familiar one at the time of the Renaissance and can be found treated by poets as far apart as Sir Philip Sidney and Andrew Marvell. In John Webster's play, *The Duchess of Malfi,* there occurs a passage strikingly similar to this poem: *Didst thou ever see a lark in a cage? Such is the soul in the body: this world is like her little turf of grass, and the heaven over our heads, like a looking glass, only gives miserable knowledge of the small compass of our prison.* (Act V, scene ii)

The poem however is far from being an academic exercise on this Platonic (rather than Christian) theme. It is, in its way, a personal allegory of Hopkins's life, bound in, albeit voluntarily, to routine and the constant thwarting of his individual and creative impulses. It suggests the extreme stress that the religious life, though willingly embraced, placed upon his life. He never wavered in his devotion, but it cost him dear, and the 'bursts of fear and rage' were buried deep in his heart, emerging as fits of depression and the torments of self-loathing that came upon him from time to time, especially in later life, finding voice in the Sonnets of Desolation.

The poem is thus personal and also prophetic. It ends characteristically, with the Resurrection hope which always shone for him, albeit sometimes with a bleak and abated light.

skylark (line 1): traditionally the bird of song, and of free soaring flight.
scanted (line 1): neglected.
bone-house, mean house (line 2): denigration of the body is more Platonic than Christian, but the expression is distinctively Hopkins's own.
beyond the remembering (line 3): i.e. having forgotten its original freedom.
This in drudgery (line 4): 'This' refers to man's mounting spirit. The laboriousness and obscurity of the religious life were themes to which Hopkins returned again and again in poems, letters and in spiritual writings. In poems as diverse and far apart as 'The Wreck of the Deutschland', 'The Windhover' and 'St Alphonsus Rodriguez' he is to be found trying to come to terms with the matter.
aloft on turf (line 5): refers to the 'turf' of clover traditionally placed in a lark's cage.
or poor low stage (line 5): either in general terms the 'stage' of life, or, more specifically, perhaps, the pulpit.

Yet both droop deadly sometimes (line 7): even in his happy early days at the seminary at St Beuno's, Hopkins was subject to the fits of weakness and melancholy which plagued him throughout life. He recorded, in a Journal entry in July 1874,

I was very tired and seemed deeply cast down till I had some kind words from the Provincial. Altogether perhaps my heart has never been so burdened and cast down as this year . . . I feel myself weak and can do little. But in all this our Lord goes his own way.

J., (249–50)

the sweet-fowl, song-fowl (line 9): the skylark in its natural state of freedom.

prison (line 11): the image of a tormented mind dashing itself against its own barriers developed in Hopkins's mind, in later years, to a type of Hell itself. See note on 'With this tormented mind', etc. in 'My own heart let me more have pity on', p. 163.

Man's spirit will be flesh-bound (line 12): he turns to his full Christian consolation. The soul will still be 'in the body' even after the individual resurrection, but the body will be glorified and immortal, no longer an encumbrance. The doctrine is fully stated in St Paul's famous Resurrection hymn in 1 Cor., xv.

meadow-down is not distressed (line 13): an analogy to convey the lightsome quality of the body after the resurrection. Man will no more be encumbered by his glorified body than meadow-down is 'distressed' by being rested upon by a rainbow-foot.

Metre: a sonnet in sprung rhythm with outriding feet, e.g.

1.4 'drudgery'; 1.8 'barriers'; 1.10 'babble and'; 1.14 'footing it'.

The rhythm is 'falling'—i.e. the stress leads each foot—and also 'paeonic' i.e. having in places *three* unstressed syllables following the stressed one, e.g. 'spirit in his' (line 2), 'remembering his' (line 3).

The Lantern out of Doors
(St Beuno's, 1877)

Written in the year of his ordination, this is one of Hopkins's 'priestly' poems in the sense that it is one of a number that he produced expressing his vocational concerns. In this case the poem is one of faith; that where human, priestly care must fail or cease when 'death or distance' intervene, the overseeing Providence of Christ has an eternal care for all men, wherever they may be.

where from, etc. (line 3): the syntax, roughly is: 'I wonder where he is from and where he is going, with his light moving along through the expanse of darkness'.

wading (line 4): suggests a light and also pushing through thick darkness. Cf. Old English *wadan* = to walk. 'Vertue gives her selfe light, through darknesse for to wade' (Spenser, *Faerie Queene*, I, i, 12).

Men go by me (line 5): general sense is that there are men, distinguished by rare gifts of body or mind, who bring 'rich beams' of light to the normal 'much-thick and marsh air' of life.

buys (line 8): i.e. swallows.

wind/What most I may eye after (lines 9–10): i.e. 'whatever object I may "wind my eyes after" I still cannot accompany it to the end, and once out of sight it is inevitably out of mind'. Bridges commented on the strangeness of the expression, and Hopkins replied, admitting that sometimes his distinctive 'inscaping' of language was prone to oddity. On this particular expression, however, he continued,

'winding the eyes' is queer only if looked at from the wrong point of view: looked at as a motion in and of the eyeballs it is what you say (i.e. queer) but I mean that the eye winds only in the sense that its focus or point of sight winds and that coincides with a point of the object and winds with that. For the object, a lantern passing further and further away and bearing now east now west of one right line, is truly and properly described as winding.

(*B*, 66–7)

Christ minds, etc. (line 12): follows by contrast from the preceding line. Though human interest fails because of death or distance Christ's redeeming Providence will pursue a man for ever. It is the same thought as in Francis Thompson's 'Hound of Heaven' though not developed so dramatically. The idea of the minute particularity of Providence in its care of the individual is not pious optimism with Hopkins, but the result of a logically articulated doctrine. In a sermon of 1880 he said:

God knows infinite things, all things, and heeds them all in particular. We cannot 'do two things at once', that is cannot give our full heed and attention to two things at once. God heeds all things at once. He takes more interest in a merchant's business than the merchant, in a vessel's steeering than the pilot, in a lover's sweetheart than the lover, in a sick man's pain than the sufferer, in our salvation than we ourselves.
(*S*, 89)

(It is interesting to note that Hopkins was 'in a manner suspended' for daring to use the word sweetheart in this sermon.)

what to avow or amend (line 12): the poet sees Christ's pursuing love as seeking always to promote the good in man and purge the evil. The whole purpose of creation to Hopkins, following Scotus, was to provide an arena for the redeeming activity of Christ. See 'The Starlight Night', note on 'the barn' (line 12).

Metre: Standard rhythm, with one sprung leading (line 12) and one line counterpointed (line 9).

The Loss of the Eurydice
(St Mary's, Chesterfield, April 1878)

Written at Chesterfield. Once again, though his muse had been 'sullen in the Sheffield, smoke-ridden air', Hopkins found himself able to write when moved by a report of a shipwreck. For a note on the inner meaning of shipwreck to Hopkins see 'The Wreck of the Deutschland', st. 1.

The poem undoubtedly has elements of oddness and eccentricity of which Hopkins himself was aware. Re-reading it one day with eyes alone (i.e. not declaiming it aloud) he confessed later that 'it struck me aghast with a kind of raw nakedness and unmitigated violence I was unprepared for' (B, 79). The Jesuit magazine The Month refused it, as it had refused 'The Wreck of the Deutschland'.

Indeed it has many faults: 1. odd and tortuous rhymes—ll.23–4, 24–5; 2. unhappy expressions—'wolfsnow', 'heavengravel', 'messes of mortals'; 3. rhetorical flatness—'there did storms not mingle?'; 4. compulsive alliteration at too great sacrifice to sense—e.g. 1.28; and 5. comic banality reminiscent of Wordsworth's weaker moments in the Lyrical Ballads, even of the owlish William McGonegall:

And he boards her in Oh! such joy
He has lost count what came next poor boy.
(ll.71–2)

Most of the glaring oddities are in the earlier part of the poem however, up to 1.73. Thereafter, it recovers itself remarkably in consistency of texture, both verbal and emotional. The wildness and strain of the first part possibly arise from insufficient data: both visually and emotionally the poet seems to be far away from immediate contact with the event. Hopkins avoided these pitfalls in 'The Wreck of the Deutschland', possibly because of the fullness of the newspaper reports available, possibly because the stark scene of the nun calling to Christ in the storm animated Hopkins's deepest feelings right from the beginning and provided a controlling perspective.

In 'The Loss of the Eurydice' it is only when he reflects on the beauty of the dead sailor and turns to religious issues that he warms to his subject. It would be difficult in this ecumenical age to share Hopkins's extreme viewpoint that because the drowned sailors were not Catholic that they were therefore in danger of damnation. But the issue was real to Hopkins, and was sufficient for poetic purposes to evoke his deep compassion and so to solemnize and steady his utterance.

In final defence, even of the oddities of the first part, one must repeat his constant plea: 'take breath and read it with the ears, as I always wish to be read, and my verse becomes all right' (*B*, 79). Add to this his great and unrequited need of an audience, and much can be forgiven him.

Metre: Sprung rhythm; 3 stresses on third line of each stanza. Other lines, 4 stresses.

Rhyme: careful rhyming, but neither eye nor voice should stop at line-endings, but rather take in a whole verse as a unit.

furled (line 6):
How are hearts of oak furled? Well, in sand and sea water . . . You are to suppose a stroke or blast in a forest of 'hearts of oak' . . . which at one blow both lays them low and buries them in broken earth.
(*B*, 52)
flockbells, etc. (lines 7–8): sheepbells off the high downs (of the Isle of Wight) knelled them to their own sea-burial.
passing measure (line 11): beyond all measure.
line 13: insistent as ever that his verse must be declaimed to the ear, not read by the eye, Hopkins said that this line 'read without stress and declaim is mere Lloyds' Shipping Intelligence; properly read it is quite a different thing. Stress is the life of it' (*B*, 52).
bole and bloom (line 16): i.e. both ship and men. Bridges objected to the poetic fitness of 'bole', but Hopkins replied that it was used by poets and also seemed 'technical and proper and in the mouth of timber merchants and so forth' (*B*, 52).
line 20: presumably scans with an accent on 'And' to make four stresses.
lines 21–2: greatly admired by Dixon, who thought them 'more English-Greek than Milton, or as much so, with more passion' (*D*, 32). The use of this exclamatory idiom causes difficulty in an age largely unacquainted with Pindaric odes.
Boreas (line 23): the north wind.
lines 23–5: . . . *wrecked her?* he/Came . . . *electric,*/*A* . . . and lines 25–6: . . . *England*/ . . . *mingle? and*
These rhymes are, to the eye alone, a comic tour de force like Byron's 'intellectual/hen-peck'd you all'. They are obviously not intended as comic, and are in fact less obtrusive when declaimed with the proper 'over-reaving' of line to line, verse to verse.
beetling baldbright, etc. (line 25): a lowering thundercloud, sharply defined and luminous at the edges.

Heavengravel (line 28): an odd word from the purely logical angle, but alliterating with 'hailropes' and 'grind'. Replaced original 'grimstones'.

wolfsnow (line 28): A rather odd usage. The adjectival prefix 'wolf' conveys emotional attitude to the snow, also alliterates with 'worlds'. The alliteration is here forced at too great a cost to the meaning.

keep (line 29): castle.

Boniface Down (line 32): above Ventnor, Isle of Wight.

Royals (line 34): sails above the topgallant. At the time of the disaster the unsuspecting ship was riding at full sail.

messes of mortals (line 40): originally 'mortholes' but still not very happy. 'I do wince a little but cannot now change it' confessed Hopkins (*B*, 53).

line 41: Bridges objected to the scanning. Hopkins replied that it is 'an anapaest, followed by a trochee, a dactyl and a syllable (*B*, 52). This would read:

$$\cup \; \cup \; - \qquad - \; \cup \qquad - \cup \; \cup \qquad -$$
Then a lurch | forward | frigate and | men.

she who (line 43): i.e. the ship.

Cheer's death (line 47): despair. The syntax reads 'Marcus Hare, her captain, stayed with her; despairing he "would" [wanted to] follow his ship to the grave'.

lines 51–2: general meaning is that he seemed to hear a voice bidding him follow his ship down.

It is even seen, etc. (line 53): 'What I say is that even those who seem unconscientious will act the right part at a great push' (*B*, 53).

line 60: metrical arrangements emphasize the speed and finality of this event.

afterdraught (line 61): the downward suction as the ship sank.

a lifebelt and God's will (line 63): to Hopkins this was possibly an example of 'novelty and boldness' (*B*, 54). To Bridges it was 'affectation' and to us it is a somewhat comic example of the figure of speech called zeugma, e.g. 'She went home in a flood of tears and a taxi.'

round air (line 65): conveys sense of light and space. Cf. Wordsworth: 'And the round ocean and the living air'.

line 73: the evocation of the handsome figure of a drowned sailor occupies Hopkins for the next three verses. Cf. 'Harry Ploughman'. Those who ascribe homosexual tendencies to Hopkins forget that an admiration for masculine beauty would be less dangerous to his priestly vows than too much description of female charms. In private notes written at Dublin he wrote briefly: 'The sight of our Lord's body is a remedy for temptation' (*S*, 255).

lines 87–8: he is led from the sinking body of the handsome sailor to think of the spiritual 'foundering' of his native people. He wrote to Patmore that 'our Empire is less and less Christian as it grows'. This to him was disastrous, as he took it that it is 'the great end of Empires before God, to be Catholic' (*FL*, 367).

born own (line 87): own born. Hopkins frequently used inversion for the sake of euphony.

I might let bygones be, etc. (line 89): from here to line 104, Hopkins is deploring the falling-off of England from the Catholic (i.e. Roman Catholic) faith since the Reformation. The argument, roughly, is: 'I would be ready to forget the evils of the past—shrines neglected, or worse still robbed, and ancient pilgrimage centres unvisited. But I must deplore human life and courage, that for example of this crew, rolled Godlessly to spiritual ruin. I am amazed that my master Christ permitted the "riving-off" [separating] of "that race" [the English] from Himself. For at one time, so near was England to the grace of God, that people who pilgrimaged by night to Walsingham would be guided by the Milky Way, calling it Walsingham Way.'

our curse (line 89): in apposition to 'bygones'.

breathing temple (line 93): still thinking of the unshrived corpse of the sailor, whose body should have been the temple of the Holy Spirit (see 1 Cor., vi, 19) but is now lost. Hopkins took a literal and extreme view of the doctrine that 'outside the Church there is no salvation'. See also Purcell sonnet.

wildworth (line 94): human qualities going to waste without the orientation which, to Hopkins, only religion can give.

in/Unchrist (lines 94–5): without knowledge of Christ, therefore to damnation, as far as Hopkins was concerned (cf. 'The Wreck of the Deutschland', st. 12, 1.5).

deplore it (line 97): i.e. so much human worth 'rolled in ruin'.

time was (line 100): at one time.

starlight-wender (line 101): any pilgrim travelling by night.

Walsingham (line 102): in Norfolk, an ancient shrine of the Virgin Mary.

And one (line 103):

The One of the Eurydice is Duns Scotus, on whom I have a sonnet lately done which I will send you. The thought is: the island was so Marian that the very Milky Way we made a roadmark to that person's shrine and from one of our seats of learning (to wit the above) went forth the first great champion of her Immaculate Conception, now in our days made an article of faith.
(*B*, 77)

For note on Duns Scotus see the sonnet mentioned, p. 87. Hopkins here interrupts himself and proceeds no further with the subject.

line 105: Hopkins here addresses all bereaved mothers, wives, sweethearts.

O well wept (line 105): 'It means "you do well to weep" and is framed like "well caught" or "well run" at a cricket match' (*B*, 53).

Wept, wife (line 106): i.e. 'O well wept, wife (also sweetheart)'.

would be one (line 106): who would have liked to have been a wife.

them (line 107): i.e. the drowned sailors.

Holiest, etc. (line 111): 'The words are put into the mouth of a mother, wife, or sweetheart who has lost a son, husband or lover respectively by the disaster' (*B*, 78).

Save my hero, O Hero savest (line 112): Hopkins concluded an involved explanation of this line to Bridges by saying that it really means 'hero of a Saviour, be the saviour of my hero' (*B*, 78).

at the awful overtaking (line 114): i.e. at the Last Judgment, hence the peculiar tense. It continues the prayer of the wife, mother or sweetheart. A paraphrase might be: 'By the time of Judgment Day, please have heard my prayer; have heard it, and granted your grace on "that day" [i.e. the day of the wreck] when grace was "wanted" [needed, also lacking]'. God's mercy, being free of the flow of time can extend 'backwards'. Hopkins's own explanation of the verb tense is attached to the Purcell sonnet, p. 89.

Last stanza (lines 117–20): the general argument is that, in Hell itself, there is no redemption even by prayer. But renewed prayer for those who seem to be in Hell (but who in fact may only be in Purgatory) will always bring the Divine pity. Hopkins is still thinking of the sailors 'in Unchrist, all rolled to ruin'. The 'doomfire' note of this stanza and of the prayer above is redolent of the hymn 'Day of Wrath' sung on 2 November, All Souls' Day, when the whole Church prays for those who have died.

The May Magnificat
(Stonyhurst, May 1878)

At Stonyhurst College, where Hopkins was staying at the time of writing this poem, it is the custom to hang verses near the statue of Mary, Mother of Christ, since May is 'Mary's month', and it is traditional to honour her at this time. This is therefore a 'Maypiece' and a public poem like 'The Silver Jubilee'.

The Magnificat is the song of praise and rejoicing ascribed to Mary in St Luke's Gospel, when she hears from Elizabeth that the babe in her womb is the Lord. It begins:
My soul magnifies[1] the Lord
and my spirit rejoices in God my Saviour.
(*RSV*, Luke, i, 56)

The poem begins by asking why May should be chosen as Mary's month. The Church has periodic celebrations ('feasts') in her honour, but there is a definite reason for their occurrence at a particular time. There seems no reason, however, for the choice of the month of May.

The rest of the poem answers the question. May is the time of blossom and fecundity in the world of nature when all life germinates and comes forth. This is 'Nature's Motherhood' upon which Mary smiles, because it recalls to her the days on earth when the child grew in her womb. There is more than that, however, and in the last four verses Hopkins raises the theme to a higher mystical level. Springtime is a 'Magnificat of nature', a hymn of earth's ecstasy which reminds Mary, now in Heaven, of her ecstasy long ago, when she knew the Babe in her womb and gave thanks to God in the words of *her* Magnificat.

Curiously enough, Hopkins did not like this beautiful little poem. Writing to Bridges, he described it as 'A Maypiece ... in which I see little good but the freedom of the rhythm' (*B*, 65). Bridges also, apparently, shared the author's misgivings, for Hopkins wrote yet again, later: 'I am not surprised at your not liking the May Magnificat which has about it something displeasing to myself' (*B*, 77).

Why did he not like it? Professor Abbott, editor of Hopkins's correspondence suggests that 'the lush yet fresh beauty of the descriptive writing which conveys the very "feel" of May-time, clashes inevitably with the praise of the Virgin Mary' (footnote to *B*, 77). W. H. Gardner disagrees, and suggests, somewhat puritanically, that Hopkins disliked the 'indecor-

[1] magnifies—*gives glory to.*

ous suggestion' in the last verse that earth has to remind Mary of her 'mirth'. Modifying Professor Abbott's view slightly, it may have been that the fecund lushness of the imagery jarred on Hopkins's deliberate and conscious asceticism at the time. His early, undergraduate poetry reveals a richly sensuous, Keatsian, strain, which he hoped he had disciplined and even renounced.

Candlemas, Lady Day (line 5): both feasts 'follow reason' in their timing. Candlemas, 2 February, celebrates the day when Mary took her babe to the Temple to 'present' him before the old priest Simeon (Luke, ii, 26). Dating from 25 December, it approximates to the interval required by ancient Jewish law (Lev., xii, 2–8) between the birth and this purifying ceremony. Since Christ, in Simeon's words, is the light of the Gentiles, the Church added a candle-ceremony to this feast day—hence Candlemas.

Lady Day is the Feast of the Annunciation, fixed by the Church exactly nine months before 25 December to celebrate the conceiving, by the Spirit, of the child in Mary's womb, the day when, in the words of Luke's gospel, 'the angel Gabriel was sent by God' to announce to Mary that she had conceived a Son not begotten of man.

Is it only, etc. (line 9): i.e. 'Is it that Mary must be delighted by the month of May merely because it is brighter than most?'

bugle blue (line 21): the bugle is the plant *ajuga reptans*, a small perennial flowering in damp woods and grassy places. It has a blue, horn-shaped blossom.

sizing (line 25): obviously put here to jingle with 'rising'. Conveys the idea of growth, to correct proportion, of each thing.

Their magnifying of each its kind (line 29): the general sense is of each thing in nature fostering and nourishing its own kind, but the line also has Scotist overtones of the intense distinctness of everything in Nature, an idea fully developed in 'As kingfishers catch fire'.

stored (line 31): this word actually qualifies 'Lord', but is luckily spaced well away from it.

Well but there was more, etc. (line 33): Hopkins raises his praise of May to a mystical level, and the imagery of spring hereafter seems to glow with an inner radiance.

drop-of-blood-and-foam-dapple (line 37): adjective qualifying 'bloom'. In his Journal of 4 May 1866 Hopkins wrote: 'Buds of apple-blossoms look like nails of blood' (*J*, 134).

thorp (line 39): a word from Old English, meaning village or field.

azuring-over greybell (line 41): i.e. the bluebell which makes a blue carpet ('azuring-over') over the greyish-brown soil of the woods.

wash wet like lakes (line 42): in his Journal of 11 May 1873 Hopkins had noticed the bluebells in Hodder wood, and the moving sea of colour they made:

the level or stage or shire of colour they make hanging in the air a foot above the grass, and a notable glare the eye may abstract and sever from the blue colour of light beating up from so many glassy heads, which like water is good to float their deeper instress on the mind.

(*J*, 231. Editor's roman.)

magic cuckoocall (line 43): through the years 1866–73 the May–June entries of Hopkins's Journal are full of references to the cuckoo. This, for instance, from 16 June 1873:

Sometimes I hear the cuckoo with wonderful clear and plump and fluty notes: it is when the hollow or a rising ground conceives them and palms them up and throws them out, like blowing into a big humming ewer—for instance under Saddle Hill one beautiful day and another time from Hodder wood when we walked on the other side of the river.

(*J*, 232)

Caps, clears and clinches all (line 44): obviously there for the alliteration, but the words also have the clear logical sense of the song dominating, soaring-over and giving pattern to the whole scene. Hopkins must have had his Stonyhurst days in mind, both here and also in the following fragment which so resembles the quotation above:

Repeat that, repeat,
Cuckoo, bird, and open ear wells, heart-springs, delightfully sweet,
With a ballad, with a ballad, a rebound
Off trundled timber and scoops of the hillside ground, hollow hollow hollow
ground:
The whole landscape flushes on a sudden at a sound.

(*Poems*, 3rd edition, 108)

Tells Mary her mirth, etc. (line 46): the syntax is 'This joy all through the earth bids [tells] Mary be reminded of her joy in the months before Christ's birth and of her "exultation" (i.e. her Magnificat)'.

Metre: Horatian stanza form similar to that employed by Andrew Marvell in his ode to Cromwell. It consists of two rhyming four-stress lines followed by two lines of three stresses, also rhyming. It has a firm structure, yet as used by Hopkins in slightly 'sprung' fashion achieves also a pleasant flexibility.

Binsey Poplars
(Oxford, March 1879)

As soon as I have time to write them out you shall have 'Duns Scotus Oxford'
(sonnet) and a little lyric 'Binsey Poplars'.
(Hopkins to Bridges, April 1879)
Hopkins's Journal is full of intensely observed 'treescapes': minute
descriptions of the texture, shape and 'lie' or the leaves, of the play of light
and shadow among branches and of the movement of wind and sun through
foliage. Above all, trees, to him, give pattern of 'inscape' to the country-
side. In a passage in his Journal written in 1873 he records precisely the
same feeling he was later to embody in this poem:
The ashtree growing in the corner of the garden was felled. It was lopped first:
I heard the sound and looking out and seeing it maimed there came at that
moment a great pang and I wished to die and not to see the inscapes of the
world destroyed any more.
(J, 230)

My aspens dear (line 1): 'I have been up to Godstow this afternoon. I am
sorry to say that the aspens that lined the river are everywhere felled' (*D*,
March 1879).
whose airy cages quelled, etc. (line 1): the thought is of the sunlight trapped
in the intricacies of leaf and branch. Hopkins described one day as 'Bright,
with a high wind blowing the crests of the trees before the sun and fetching
in the blaze and dousing it again' (*J*, 233).
the leaping sun (line 2): Hopkins one day described the sun above wood-
land trees at St Beuno's as 'a shaking white fire or waterball, striking and
glanting' (*J*, 239).
sandalled Shadow (lines 6–7): the adjective carries multiple association, e.g.
soft, stealthy and interlaced.
that swam (line 7): i.e. the shadow.
wind-wandering, etc. (line 8): strong suggestion through onomatopoeia of
the dreamy, meandering river. Cf. similar effects in a passage in Joyce's
Finnegan's Wake (p. 216):
Beside the rivering waters of, the hitherandthithering waters of. Night.
unselve (line 21): annihilate the identity of.
especial (line 22): in the Scotist sense of unique, never to be repeated.

Metre: Lines are of variable stress. Number of stresses can be calculated
by how much the line is indented, e.g. ll.1–8 as follows 5–5–5–4–2–2–3–6.

Duns Scotus's Oxford
(March 1879)

Duns Scotus: thirteenth-century philosopher and an important influence on Hopkins. See Introduction, p. 21.

Towery city (line 1): cf. Arnold, 'city of dreaming spires'. Cf. too Hopkins's early poem 'To Oxford' (1865):

Those charms accepted of my inmost thought
The towers musical, quiet-walled groves.

line 2: a line at once melodious, yet jangling, inscaping the sights and sounds of Oxford.

bell-swarmed (line 2): cf. 'The air swarmed with bells on the hour', Aileen Ward describing Keats's visit to Oxford (*John Keats*, Secker [London, 1963], p. 127).

coped and poisèd powers (line 4): the influences (or atmospheres) of town and country set off and balanced, one against the other.

base and brickish skirt (line 5): a circle of dreary suburban building round the original city.

sours (line 5): i.e. that sours. Hopkins wrote to Dixon of 'that landscape the charm of Oxford, green shouldering grey, which is already abridged and soured and perhaps will soon be put out altogether' (*D*, 20).

Graceless growth (line 7): i.e. the 'base and brickish skirt'.

confounded/Rural rural keeping (lines 7-8): the word 'keeping' to Hopkins meant 'distinctive atmosphere'. Writing about William Barnes the rural Dorset poet, he said:

It is his naturalness that strikes me most; he is like an embodiment or incarnation or manmuse of the country, of Dorset, of rustic life and humanity. He comes, like Homer and all poets of native epic, provided with epithets, images, and so on which seem to have been tested and digested for a long age in their native air and circumstances and to have a keeping which nothing else could give.

(*FL*, 370)

He haunted (line 11): Duns Scotus studied, and later lectured, at Oxford.

sways my spirits to peace (line 11): because Scotus vindicated the reality and certainty of knowledge that comes through the senses. Hopkins needed the vindication because otherwise he would have felt the obligation to accept the overwhelming authority of St Thomas Aquinas, who taught that sense-knowledge is not knowledge at all. This would have undoubtedly caused severe conflict in Hopkins who felt instinctively the validity and beauty of that which comes to us via the senses. See Introduction, p. 21.

realty (line 12): reality.

rarest-veinèd unraveller (line 12): Scotus was noted for the subtlety of his distinctions, in his philosophical analysis of experience.

Italy (line 13): home of St Thomas Aquinas, greatest of the thirteenth-century scholastic philosophers. The works of St Thomas still enjoy an almost canonical authority in the Catholic Church.

Greece (line 13): ancient Greece, the fountain and source of Western philosophy, notably in Plato and Aristotle.

fired France for Mary without spot (line 14): against St Thomas and others, Duns Scotus upheld the doctrine of the Immaculate Conception of Mary. Immaculate = *sine macula* = without stain. The doctrine is that Mary the mother of Christ was a chosen vessel and was born free of stain of Original Sin which the rest of the human race had inherited from the Fall—the 'fall', i.e. from original obedience to God into slavery to self. The doctrine was finally defined as obligatory and 'of faith' to Catholics by Pope Pius IX in 1854.

Hopkins in one of his sermons refers to a great debate at the University of Paris, when Scotus, 'this wise and happy man . . . broke the objections brought against him as Samson broke the thongs and withies with which his enemies had tried to bind him' (*N*, 269).

Metre: A sonnet in sprung rhythm with many 'outriding' feet, e.g. 'echoing' (line 2), 'swarmed' (line 2), 'below thee' (line 3), 'encounter in' (line 4), etc.

Henry Purcell
(Oxford, April 1879)

Shortly after writing this sonnet, Hopkins was forced, at the request of Bridges, to explain a number of points in it. Four years later, in 1883, probably after another request for clarification, he sent Bridges a complete prose 'argument'. 'It is somewhat dismaying', he wrote, 'to find I am so unintelligible though, especially in one of my very best pieces' (*B*, 171).

The main obscurities are:

1. the somewhat irrelevant piece of religious legalism in lines 3–4.
2. the development of a Scotist concept of 'self hood' in lines 5–8.
3. a complicated and rather clumsy analogy in the sestet, which Hopkins himself admitted was not so clearly worked out as he could wish (see *B*, 83).

These difficulties will be discussed in the commentary. It was the knowledge of their presence which probably impelled Hopkins to fix the short explanation printed at the top of the poem. The words 'very make and species' convey what we would mean by 'the very essence'.

Henry Purcell: 1659–95, organist at Westminster and at the Chapel Royal, composer-in-ordinary to the king, and the greatest of a great family of English musicians. He was a composer of extraordinary versatility, producing works of rare distinction and originality for a variety of occasions. Some of his technical usages have influenced twentieth-century composers, and it is not surprising, therefore, to find him being admired by Hopkins, who in technical matters was also far in advance of his time and a formative influence on some twentieth-century poets.

Have fair fallen (line 1): i.e. may a fair fortune have befallen you. There is a similar usage in lines 113–16 of 'The Loss of the Eurydice'. On the tense of the verb Hopkins wrote:

It is the singular imperative (or optative if you like) of the past, a thing possible and actual both in logic and grammar, but naturally a rare one. As in the second person we say 'Have done' or in making appointments 'Have had your dinner beforehand', so one can say in the third person not only 'Fair fall' of what is present or future but also 'Have fair fallen' of what is past. (*B*, 174)

arch-especial (line 2): utterly distinctive. The word 'special' would carry for Hopkins, the meaning given to it by his beloved Scotus (Introduction, p. 21) who used the concept of *species specialissima* to denote the completely distinctive reality of each act of awareness, and of the object conveyed in that act.

with the reversal (line 3): i.e. together with the reversal of 'the heavy con-
demnation under which he outwardly or nominally lay for being out of the
true Church' (*B*, 171).

listed to (line 4): i.e. enlisted under. The whole idea of Purcell's being listed
to a heresy' (Protestantism) and therefore being in danger of eternal
damnation is typical of the Ultramontane severity of Hopkins's interpretation of the Trent doctrine 'Outside the Church there is no salvation',
promulgated at the time of the Reformation. It can be seen elsewhere in
'The Wreck of the Deutschland' and 'The Loss of the Eurydice' where he
mourns that the victims were mostly non-Catholics and therefore probably
damned. This rigid view was prevalent at the time, but Hopkins would
certainly have had to revise it in the light of later official condemnations of
this too exclusivist attitude.

Not mood in him nor meaning, etc. (line 5): the general argument of these
next four lines was supplied by Hopkins:

*I love his genius . . . not so much for the gifts he shares, even though it shd. be
in higher measure, with other musicians as for his own individuality.*
(*B*, 170)

fire . . . fear . . . love . . . pity, etc. (lines 5–6): the possible emotions that any
composer might be expected to 'nursle' or evoke in the hearer.

forgèd feature finds me (line 7): i.e. it is the individual stamp on his music
that really moves me. 'So that while he is aiming only at impressing me
his hearer with the meaning in hand I am looking out meanwhile
for his specific, his individual markings and mottlings, "the sakes of
him" (ibid.).

it is the rehearsal/Of own, of abrupt self, etc. (lines 7–8): i.e. it is the revelation of personal and unique individuality conveyed through the music that
so 'thrusts on' (makes such an impact on) and so 'throngs' (crowds in upon
and takes possession of) the hearer. In a meditation, Hopkins had written
of self-consciousness as the being aware of a 'throng and stack of being,
so rich, so distinctive, so important' (*S*, 122). Purcell, in addition to the
other qualities of his music, inimitably conveys through it the 'throng and
stack' of his own being, charming the ear of Hopkins.

Have an eye to the sakes of him (line 10): i.e. 'I will watch out for the unique
"Henry Purcell" qualities in the music'. Hopkins had used the word 'sake'
in 'The Wreck of the Deutschland', st. 22. He explained its use here to
Bridges:

*Sake is a word I find it convenient to use . . . I mean by it the being a thing has
outside itself, as a voice by its echo, a face by its reflection, a body by its
shadow . . .* and also *that in the thing by virtue of which especially it has this
being abroad, and that is something distinctive, marked, specifically or*

individually speaking ... *In this case it is, as the sonnet says, distinctive quality in genius.*
(*B*, 83. Hopkins's roman)
quaint moonmarks (line 10): the moonmarks are 'crescent-shaped markings on the quillfeathers'. They belong to the simile which Hopkins only properly introduces in the next line.
to his pelted, etc. (line 10): i.e. have an eye to his pelted, etc.
whenever he has walked his while/The thunder-purple seabeach, etc. (lines 11–12): the sense is 'whenever some great stormfowl, himself with purple-of-thunder plumage, has walked his while on the thunder-purple seabeach'.
wuthering (line 13): 'Wuthering', explained Hopkins, 'is a Northcountry word for the noise and rush of the wind: hence Emily Brontë's *Wuthering Heights*' (*B*, 83). W. H. Gardner elucidates a network of association—a passage from *Wuthering Heights* and a passage from Hopkins's own Journal—that went into this section of the poem (*WHG*, Vol. II, 279–80).
colossal smile (line 13): in the sense of a sudden radiance as he spreads his feathers and reveals the glory of his plumage.
but meaning motion (line 14): i.e. meaning merely to move. Although he is beating his wings merely to start flight he also 'fans fresh' the mind of the observer with the splendour of his markings. Hopkins explained, somewhat laboriously:
The thought is that as the seabird opening his wings with a whiff of wind in your face means the whirr of the motion, but also unaware gives you a whiff of knowledge about his plumage, the marking of which stamps his species, that he does not mean, so Purcell, seemingly intent only on the thought or feeling he is to express or call out, incidentally lets you remark the individualizing marks of his own genius.
(*B*, 83)

Metre: A sonnet in Alexandrines, i.e. six stresses per line. It is in sprung rhythm, with many outriding feet. Hopkins believed that Alexandrine 'unless broken, as I do, by outrides, is very tedious' (*B*, 80). W. H. Gardner lists the outriding feet as follows, marked with the customary nether loop:

1.1 *have fallen.* 1.2. *To me.* 1.4. *sentence ... listed* 1.5. *meaning.*

1.6 *all that* 1.8. *self there ... thrusts on.* 1.9. *angels ... lay me.*

1.10. *sakes of him ... moonmarks.* 1.11. *stormfowl.*

1.13. *wuthering of his palmy snow-pinions.* 1.14. *Off him ... motion.*

(Notes to Penguin edition, p. 231)

The Candle Indoors
(Oxford, 1879)

'A companion to the Lantern, not at first meant to be though, but it fell in', wrote Hopkins to Bridges (*B*, 84). In this sonnet the priest passes by a window, a candle burning within. He hopes devoutly that whoever is working there, inside, is giving due glory to God. In the sestet he rebukes himself for these idle speculations, and bids himself tend his own inner resources of faith ('vital candle in close heart's vault'). Bridges must have protested against some (to him) unlikelihood in the situation, drawing from Hopkins the reply that 'though the analogy in the Candle sonnet may seem forced, yet it is an "autobiographical" fact that I was influenced and acted on the way there said' (*B*, 85).

somewhere I come by (line 1): a typical ellipse. Could mean either, 'as I come by' or 'some place that I pass'.

puts blissful back (line 2): general sense is that the yellow candle-light peacefully pushes back the darkness.

to-fro tender trambeams (line 4): the delicate lines of light which seem to dart from a source of light to the eyelashes. They can best be seen when the eye is half closed.

truckle at (line 4): verb meaning 'subservient to', i.e. responding to the slightest movement of the eyelashes, receding or lengthening as the eye is opened or closed.

By that window, etc. (lines 5–8): general sense of the syntax is 'As I plod by the window I wonder what hands are working inside. Simply because I do not know, I am all the more anxious that whatever man or woman ("Jessy or Jack") is inside should be working for God's glory.'

There/(line 8): the stroke (or space) immediately after this word is to denote a pause.

Come you indoors, come home (line 9): an injunction addressed to himself to mind his own business and to give God glory in his own life instead of worrying about what others are doing.

your fading fire, etc. (lines 9–10): both 'fading fire' and 'vital candle' are objects of imperative 'mend'. Both metaphors refer to the inner energies of faith and love, without which nothing can be accomplished for God.

beam-blind (line 12): blind to your own faults. The whole trend of thought brings the poet to Christ's command 'Judge not, that ye be not judged' and the words which follow:

Or how wilt thou say to thy brother, Let me pull the mote out of thine eye; and behold a beam is in thine own eye.

Thou hypocrite, first cast out the beam out of thine own eye; and then thou shalt see clearly to cast out the mote out of thy brother's eye.
(Matt., vii, *AV*)

deft-handed (line 13): i.e. quick to seize upon. Hopkins is still thinking in terms of Christ's metaphor of a hand too ready to pluck out the 'mote' (fault, blind spot) in someone else's eye.

liar (line 13): i.e. the hypocrite referred to in the quotation.

spendsavour salt (line 14): an echo of Matt., v, 13, where Christ calls his disciples the salt of the earth and warns them not to lose their savour. Salt that has exhausted its savour is 'thenceforth good for nothing, but to be cast out, and to be trodden under foot of men'.

The whole section is an admonition by Hopkins to himself to safeguard his spiritual energies. Periods of acute exhaustion and depression were in fact to be a feature of his priestly life—see the Sonnets of Desolation and, especially, the introduction to them, p. 145.

Metre: Standard sonnet rhythm—i.e. 5 iambic feet (1 'foot' = 1 unstressed followed by 1 stressed syllable) per line. The rhythm however is counter-pointed—see metre note on 'God's Grandeur', pp. 55–6.

The Handsome Heart
(Oxford, 1879)

Hopkins recast this poem twice. He sent the first version (A.1) to Bridges, in June 1879, together with 'The Candle Indoors' saying that both poems were 'capable of further finish' and 'not very good all through'.

Bridges, to Hopkins's surprise, liked it, and asked Hopkins to revise it. This was done and version A.2 appeared. Hopkins later recast the poem again into six-stress lines (version B), which according to Bridges lacked charm and freshness, had an awkward emendation and also contained seven 'what's.

So Bridges finally printed A.1, plus a few emendations which is the official version.

It was written, along with 'The Bugler's First Communion', and others, during Hopkins's year as a priest at Oxford, December 1878–October 1879 (see notes on 'The Bugler's First Communion'). Hopkins described the incident to Bridges as follows:

The story was that last Lent, when Fr. Parkinson was laid up in the country, two boys of our congregation gave me much help in the sacristy in Holy Week. I offered them money for their services, which the elder refused, but being pressed consented to take it laid out in a book. The younger followed suit: then when some days after I asked him what I shd. buy answered as in the sonnet.
(*B*, 86)

The philosophy behind it is that just as beauty of the mind is greater than physical beauty, so beauty of character is greater than either. Hopkins expressed it to Bridges in a letter of October the same year, as follows:

I think then that no one can admire beauty of the body more than I do, and it is of course a comfort to find beauty in a friend, or a friend in beauty. But this kind of beauty is dangerous.[1] *Then comes beauty of the mind, such a genius, and this is greater than the beauty of the body and not to call dangerous. And more beautiful than the beauty of the mind is beauty of character, the 'handsome heart'.*
(*B*, 95)

'Father, what you buy me', etc. (line 2): This is the child's reply to Father Hopkins.
With the sweetest air that said, etc. (lines 3–4): these two lines, very loosely paraphrased, read, 'This was the child's sweet reply and, though continually

---

[1] Cf. *'To What Serves Mortal Beauty'*.

pressed to make his own choice, he stuck to his first, considered answer.'
like carriers let fly (line 5): i.e. like carrier pigeons released. He had used the
same simile in 'The Wreck of the Deutschland', st. 3.
Doff darkness, etc. (line 6): put aside or ignore the darkness and trust to
their unerring instinct. The poet is saying that the heart has an instinct
for what is good, and if unhindered will go that way. In other places he is
not as optimistic as this about natural goodness.
self-instressed (line 7): behaving according to its own nature. See Introduction, pp. 28–9.
Falls light, etc. (line 8): the heart, if left alone, falls as naturally into the
paths of goodness as if it had had ten years' training. Hopkins is perhaps
thinking of his own arduous Jesuit training, not finished even at this stage,
and comparing it to this boy's natural goodness.
more than handsome face (line 9): see introduction above.
Beauty's bearing or muse, etc. (line 10): the 'handsome heart' is of more
value than beauty or than poetic genius. Hopkins illustrated this thought,
further, to Bridges as follows:

*. . . there may be genius uninformed by character. I sometimes wonder at this
in a man like Tennyson: his gift of utterance is truly golden, but go further
home and you come to thoughts commonplace and wanting in nobility (it
seems hard to say it but I think you know what I mean). In Burns there is
generally recognized on the other hand a richness and beauty of manly
character which lends worth to some of his smallest fragments, but there is a
great want in his utterance.*
(*B*, 95)

Of heaven what boon (line 12): really a question the priest puts to himself:
'What good thing can I ask heaven to give you that you have not got
already?' The answer follows.
Only . . . O on that path you pace (line 13): i.e. I pray heaven only that you
remain on that path, etc. The 'O' is part of the fervour of the prayer.
Hopkins informed Bridges that 'The little hero of the Handsome Heart is
gone to school at Boulogne to be bred for a priest and he is bent on being a
Jesuit' (*B*, 92).
brace sterner than strain (line 14): i.e. 'bend all your energies behind that
willed movement of your being (toward God)'. In a retreat at Beaumont in
1878, Hopkins had discovered the works of a nineteenth-century French
nun, Marie Lataste, who had written that there are too 'strains' or move-
ments-of-being in man, 'that of his being created by God, and that of his
existing being towards God' (Father Devlin's translation, *S*, 289, note). The
first movement—i.e. into existence—is of course involuntary; but the
second, the movement towards God, has to be willed and chosen. It is a

'strain' both in the sense of movement-of-being-towards, and also of hard effort. Of this willed effort to move forwards towards God, Hopkins wrote: *It cuts off the flowing skirts of idleness and worldliness, a spreading of ourselves and of our being out on lower things, and* braces, binds us fast into God's service.
(Sermon Notes, October 1879, *S*, 234, Editor's roman)

Metre: Standard rhythm counterpointed, i.e. subtle irregularities of stress (e.g. lines 7–8) mounted on a basic iambic pentameter.

The Bugler's First Communion
(Oxford, (?) 27 July 1879)

Apart from a short stay at the fashionable Jesuit Church at Farm Street, London, Hopkins's first real post, after his ordination, was at Oxford, where he spent nearly a year. During this first brief spell of priestly duties he wrote several priestly poems. 'I find within my professional experience now a good deal of matter to write on,' he wrote to Bridges (*B*, 86). The poems included 'The Brothers', 'The Handsome Heart' and 'The Bugler's First Communion'.

He did not get on very well at Oxford. After he had left, and gone to Leigh in Lancashire, he wrote to Bridges:

However it is perhaps well I am gone; I did not quite hit it off with Fr Parkinson and was not happy. I was fond of my people, but they had not as a body the charming and cheering heartiness of these Lancashire Catholics, which is so deeply comforting: they were far from having it. And I believe they criticized what went on in our church a great deal too freely, which is a d——d impertinence of the sheep towards the Shepherd, and if it had come markedly before me I shd. have given them my mind.
(*B*, 97)

This poem, however, reflects none of this disillusion. It arises out of Hopkins's duties as Chaplain to Cowley Barracks. It uses military metaphors, suitable both to the subject, a young bugler-boy at his first communion, and to the poet himself, gained in a religious order run on para-military lines. It expresses the hopes and fears of the priest-poet as he contemplates the youth and innocence of the young communicant. He is anxious that the youth should remain a true soldier of Christ, pure and unstained by the world. The somewhat morbid lengths to which Hopkins took this sentiment may be gathered from a note to Bridges: 'I enclose a poem, the Bugler. I am half inclined to hope the Hero of it may be killed in Afghanistan' (*B*, 92). At the end of his MS of the sonnet, he wrote: 'Ordered to Mootlan [Mooltan] in the Punjaub; was to sail Sept. 30.'

Neither Bridges nor the average reader could readily be expected to share either Hopkins's life-denying otherworldliness or his too-innocent idealisms compounded of eager patriotism, knightly chivalry and a romanticized notion of sexual purity. Yet behind this apparent naivety there lies a passionately held religious philosophy,

1. that the lost kingdom of innocence still lies in our hearts and can occasionally be seen in the face of youth
2. that to such a world of innocence, if man had not fallen, Christ would

have come, not as a poor man to be crucified, but in his true splendour as King and High Priest (see Father Devlin's Introduction to the Sermons, *S*, 6)

3. that all baptized and confirmed Christians are 'knights' of Christ 'and having been knighted are bound by allegiance, fealty, loyalty, chivalry' (*S*, 163)

This fervent idealism then has deep roots in Duns Scotus's theory of the Incarnation and in St Ignatius's soul-challenging view of the Christian life as a call to warfare.

This poem is a fascinating piece of language. It ranges from the easy colloquialism of the first stanza, through the playful tongue-twisting of stanza 7, to the hard cryptic inversions of the final verse. It is full of pleasurable things like 'Forth Christ from cupboard fetched, how fain I of feet', and 'Those sweet hopes quell whose least me quickenings lift'. The rhymes occasionally *look* eccentric (e.g. st. 1, st. 2) but since the lines are 'overrove' (drawn out into one another) and the poem, like all Hopkins's poems, is meant to be read aloud, this is not a great obstacle.

boon he on/My late being there begged, etc. (lines 5–6): Hopkins had to explain to Bridges:
The words . . . mean 'came into Oxford to our Church in quest of (or to get) a blessing which, on a late occasion of my being up at Cowley Barracks, he had requested of me': there is no difficulty here, I think.
(*B*, 97)

boon he on . . . Communion (lines 5 and 8): this rhyme, like 'Irish . . . sire he sh[ares]' looks odd. Bridges must have protested, but Hopkins wrote: 'I cannot stop to defend the rhymes in the Bugler' (*B*, 97).

In his Preface to his notes to the first edition (1918), Bridges returned to the attack:
Gerard Hopkins, where he is simple and straightforward in his rhyme is as master of it—there are many instances—but when he indulges in freaks, his childishness is incredible . . . The rhyme to 'communion' in 'The Bugler' is hideous, and the suspicion that the poet thought it ingenious is appalling.
(op. cit., p. 98)

Bridges was subsequently taken to task by later editors of Hopkins's poems, such as Charles Williams and W. H. Gardner.

how fain I of feet (line 10): i.e. how quick and eager to bring Christ in Communion to this boy.

his youngster (line 11): i.e. Christ's youngster.

his treat (line 11): Christ's 'treat' is the gift of Himself in the bread of Communion.

Low-latched in leaf-light housel (line 12): 'housel' is an archaic word for the Communion wafer, which, according to Roman Catholic doctrine, *is* Christ present under the appearance of bread. Hopkins imagines Christ as humbly enclosed or locked away in this 'leaf-light' wafer.

There (line 13): the priest puts the wafer on the boy's tongue and then prays for him.

and your sweetest sendings, etc. (line 13): the sense is 'By this Communion, may Heaven send its sweetest blessings on this youth'. He gives examples of such blessings—a brave heart, a tongue not given to boasting and scorn ('vaunt- and tauntless'), and the living glow ('breathing bloom') of chastity.

angel-warder (line 17): the belief in a personal guardian-angel was, and still is to some extent, an item of popular Catholic piety. A year after writing this poem, Hopkins preached a whole sermon on the subject at Liverpool:

... in appointing us guardian angels God never meant they should make us proof against all the ills that flesh is heir to, that would have been to put us in some sort back into the state of Paradise which we have lost; but he meant them, accompanying us through this world of evil and mischance, sometimes warding off its blows and buffets, sometimes leaving them to fall, always to be leading us to a better: which better world, my brethren, when you have reached and with your own eyes opened look back on this you will see a work of wonderful wisdom in the guidance of your guardian angel.

(S, 92)

Squander (line 18): scatter, disintegrate. Cf. similar use of the word in 'Heraclitean Fire'.

hell-rook ranks sally to molest (line 18): i.e. the ranks (that) come forth from Hell to molest, etc. In an Ignatian meditation, Jesuits are advised to imagine Satan sending his evil forces abroad upon the world:

... consider how he summons together innumerable devils, and how he disperses them, some to one city, some to another, and so on throughout the whole world, omitting no province, place or state of life, nor any person in particular.

('The Two Standards', printed in S, 178)

kind comrade (line 19): i.e. the guardian angel.

dexterous and starlight order (line 20): one of the magic phrases that remain in the mind. It is impossible to translate literally, but it implies a life of peace and order lived close to the eternal will of God, not enmeshed or bemired in sin.

tread tufts of consolation (line 25): the image communicates a springy walk above the bog of depression which always threatened Hopkins. The light-hearted playing on words in the next two lines adds to the effect.

royal ration (line 28): the Bread, which is Christ himself.

not all so strains/Us (lines 29–30): the sense is that nothing moves him more to priestly care and fervour than the sight of 'fresh youth', for the sight of such bloom and freshness is a symbol of 'that sweet's sweeter ending', the Paradise of Heaven.

that sealing sacred ointment (line 33): the priest's hands, with which he administers the Sacraments and blessings of the Church, are, at his ordination, anointed with ointment and then bound together, to symbolize their being set apart for Christ's work on earth. Hopkins hopes that his priestly ministrations will prove a shield and defence for the boy.

what bans off bad (line 34): i.e. whatever is effective in warding off evil.

Let me though see no more of him, etc. (line 36): a surprising sentiment, but the reason follows: he could not stand the thought of the boy being untrue to Christ, and the dashing of those hopes whose least stirring give him joy ('whose least me quickenings lift') of one day finding a true knight of Christ.

In scarlet or somewhere (line 38): his hopes of finding a 'Galahad' for Christ are not necessarily confined to the bugler boy.

That brow and bead of being (line 39): that consummation of human perfection. Lying behind this metaphor, with its overtones of Christ's agony and blood-sweat in Gethsemane (Luke, xxiv, 44) is a network of association that takes us into the deeper levels of Hopkins's thinking. The perfection of human nature, according to Hopkins, is the sacrificial self and the highest and most distinctive 'self' is that which is capable of voluntary self-sacrifice or oblation. Christ, on the eve of his total sacrifice, sweated beads of blood from his brow. This same sacrificial 'strain' which He showed to humanity, in a human way, goes on, in an inexpressible way, in the inner life of the Trinity in an eternal 'blissful agony' of love and creative self-giving. 'It is as if the blissful agony or stress of selving in God had forced out drops of sweat or blood, which drops were the world' (Long Retreat Notes, 1881—*S*, 197). Hence the association of 'brow and bead' with self-giving, and the highest forms of human perfection.

An our day's God's own Galahad (line 40): i.e. a modern-day Galahad whose life is devoted to the service of God. Sir Galahad was a knight of Arthurian legend, fierce in battle, chivalrous and chaste. As may be seen from 'The Windhover' and the last line of 'The Wreck of the Deutschland', the notions of honour and chivalry were closely connected in Hopkins's mind with the service of God. St Ignatius, founder of the Jesuit order, wrote of Baptism and Confirmation as a call to arms, to knightly service of Christ the King (see text in *S*, 160). Hopkins meditated upon this as follows:

. . . *the king's call is to those directly who have already committed themselves to something, are* equites *(remark the word), knights, follow the profession of arms and having been knighted are bound by allegiance, fealty, loyalty, chivalry,* knighthood *in a word, to live up to a standard of courage above the civilian and even above the private soldier. And an adult Christian is such, being not only baptized but confirmed (for Confirmation is spiritual knighthood).*

(Hopkins's notes on 'De Christo Rege', *S*, 163, Hopkins's roman)

Though this child's drift, etc. (line 40): the thought is that the lad's life is already fixed by his choice of military profession, though this is no necessary disaster to his religious development.

may he not rankle and roam (line 42): one final fear expressed that the boy though 'bound home' (ultimately destined for Heaven), may be tempted to wander from the straight and narrow path of salvation.

That left to the Lord, etc. (line 44): i.e. 'having left that final fear in God's hands, I hereby lay the matter aside'. The Eucharist is the Communion Wafer, in which Christ, in Roman doctrine, makes Himself present.

Recorded only (line 45): i.e. 'so long as it will be recorded that I have uttered pleas that would shake Heaven', etc.

brandle (line 46): obsolete word for 'shake'.

ride and jar (line 46): i.e. assault and clash, taking the kingdom of Heaven by storm.

Forward-like, but however, etc. (line 48): an involved, elliptical piece of syntax, triumphally final, and almost comparable to the flourish at the end of 'The Wreck of the Deutschland'. The sense is 'But, however, all this worry is premature and presumptuous ('forward-like') and in all probability ('like' = belike) Heaven was favourable to these prayers'.

Metre: Sprung rhythm, overrove, with an 'outrider' between the 3rd and 4th foot of the 4th line in each stanza.

Morning Midday and Evening Sacrifice
(Oxford, August 1879)

The conviction of the life-giving power of self-sacrifice was very central to Hopkin's thinking—see note on 'brow and bead of being', line 39 of 'The Bugler's First Communion'. This poem represents the three stages of life, all of which must be given to Christ, the bloom of youth, the strength and maturity of mid-years and the wisdom of age.

Dixon liked this poem, and in 1886, having been asked by Routledge the publishers to edit a Bible Birthday Book, asked Hopkins if he could use the first stanza. Hopkins consented (with the usual provisos about permission from superiors and the need for anonymity) and the verse was printed, with minor changes, under 25 May, with the text: 'As for the oblation of the first fruits, ye shall offer them unto the Lord' (Lev., ii, 12).

Stanza 1
die-away (line 1): could mean either the gentle curving of the cheek, or the pink, blending or 'dying'—into the white.
wimpled (line 2): delicately curved.
all this, beauty blooming (line 5): in a sermon of 31 August 1879, exactly contemporary with the writing of this poem, Hopkins said:
. . . the man or woman, the boy or girl, that in their bloom and heyday, in their strength and health give themselves to God and with the fresh body and joyously beating blood give him glory, how near he will be to them in age and sickness and wall their weakness round in the hour of death.
(*S*, 19)
See also the last line of 'Spring', when he asks Christ to claim the 'innocent mind and Mayday in girl and boy' before it goes 'sour with sinning'.
fuming (line 6): the metaphor is from incense, a sweet-smelling gum that glows and smokes when lit and swung gently in a censer, an ornate metal bowl suspended on a light chain. It is used in liturgical rites as a visible symbol of human prayer and sacrifice ascending to God. Hopkins saw the whole world as a censer breathing adoration to its creator:
It is a censer fuming: what is the sweet incense? His praise, his reverence, his service; it rises to his glory. It is an altar and a victim on it lying in his sight: why is it offered? To his praise, honour, and service: it is a sacrifice to his glory.
(Notes on 'The Principle or Foundation', *S*, 238)
He was, however, to add about sinful, fallen humanity, 'Are we his censer? we breathe stench and not sweetness' (*S*, 240).

Stanza 2

Both thought and thew now bolder (line 1): Hopkins passes to the state of maturity when mind and body ('thew' = muscle) are fully developed.
Tower (line 2): i.e. be exultant in your strength. The command is given by Nature.
Take as for tool, not toy meant (line 6): in his notes on 'The Principle or Foundation' quoted above, Hopkins also wrote:
When a man is in God's grace and free from mortal sin, then everything that he does, so long as there is no sin in it, gives God glory . . . It is not only prayer that gives God glory but work. Smiting on an anvil, sawing a beam, white-washing a wall, driving horses, sweeping, scouring, everything gives God some glory if being in his grace you do it as your duty.
(*S*, 240)

Stanza 3

vault and scope (line 1): in words which have Shakespearian echoes suggesting a past life of ambition, action and achievement, Hopkins turns to the period of old age, when life is lived chiefly in the mind.
mastery in the mind (line 2): Hopkins is here speaking of that self-mastery in the service of God, often achieved only after a lifetime's struggle. 'You cannot mean your praise if while praise is on the lips there is no reverence in the mind; there can be no reverence in the mind if there is no obedience, no submission, no service' (Notes on 'The Principle or Foundation', *S*, 240)
In silk-ash kept from cooling (line 3): the original version was 'Silk-ashed but core not cooling' by which Hopkins meant to convey grey hairs concealing a mind and brain glowing with love of God. He wrote to Bridges:
. . . the line 'Silk-ashed' etc in the Sacrifice is too hard and must be changed to 'In silk-ash kept from cooling'. I meant to compare grey hairs to the flakes of silky ash which may be seen round wood embers burnt in a clear fire and covering a 'core of heat' as Tennyson calls it. But 'core' there is very ambiguous.
(*B*, 97–8)
In 'The Windhover' he used a similar image of a glowing core of heat under dead-looking embers to describe the religious life.
Your offering, with despatch, of (line 7): Hopkins explained:
'Your offer, with despatch, of' is said like 'Your ticket', 'Your reasons', 'Your money or your life', 'Your name and college'; it is 'Come, your offer of all this (the matured mind), and without delay either'.
(*B*, 98)
This explains the preceding two lines. The matured mind is that which 'hell stalks towards the snatch of'. The earlier version, perhaps clearer, was,

What death half lifts the latch of,
What hell hopes soon the snatch of,
This latter reading has been restored in the fourth edition.

Hopkins believed, quite literally, that a man who died suddenly, in his sins, without opportunity for repentance, would be eternally damned.

Metre: 'As befits the theme', writes W. H. Gardner, 'the metrical unit is the most solemn in English verse—the trimeter' (*WHG*, Vol. II, 288).

Andromeda
(Oxford, 12 August 1879)

The Greek legend of Andromeda: the god Perseus, fresh from his conquest of the Gorgon Medusa, was winging his way across Africa, when he came upon a beautiful girl chained to a black rock on the edge of the sea. Her name was Andromeda, daughter of a king, and she was about to be offered as a sacrifice, to propitiate a devouring sea monster that was ravaging the coast. Perseus killed the monster, freed the girl and later married her.

The Perseus myth was a favourite with nineteenth-century writers and artists. Charles Kinglsey wrote his 'Andromeda' on the theme, and artists such as Burne-Jones (a friend of Dixon's), Ingres and Lord Leighton interpreted it on canvas. There are a number of fairly definite visual details in the poem—the 'rock rude', the 'horns of shore' and the picture of Perseus hovering over the scene—but there is no evidence that Hopkins had any particular picture in mind.

The legend is readily adaptable, for Hopkins's poetic and religious purposes. Andromeda, in this sonnet, is the Church on earth, the Bride of Christ, persecuted and afflicted throughout time. Perseus is Christ, the Bridegroom, the Saviour and Spouse of the Church, seemingly absent from her as she suffers in patience, but finally descending to conquer the evils that beset her. This 'apocalyptic' imagery of suffering and victory, in terms of fight against a great beast, is to be found in the Book of Revelation.

Time's Andromeda (line 1): because the Church on earth is perpetually suffering throughout time.

this rock rude (line 1): the Church is founded upon the 'rock' of Peter (see Matt., xvi, 18), but the rock here is referred to is probably the planet earth itself to which the suffering Church is bound.

With not her either beauty's equal, etc. (lines 2–3): with nothing to equal her either in beauty or in the ravages she has suffered. The inversion and compression of the word-order produces a harmonious 'inscape' of sound and meaning, where the normal phrase would have been verbose and awkward.

doomed dragon's food (line 4): in his Long Retreat Notes of 1881, Hopkins wrote of dragons as gathering up the attributes of many creatures:

I suppose the dragon as a type of the Devil to express the universality of his powers, both the gifts he has by nature and the attributes and sway he grasps, and the horror which the whole inspires.

(*S*, 199)

In the same passage, he also wrote:

And I cannot help suspecting that the attack on the woman which the dragon makes was, though I cannot yet clearly grasp how, the actual attack which he made, is making, and will go on making on the human race.

(*S*, 200)

The poem, of course, is of earlier date than these notes, but both reflect the same imagery.

attempted (line 5): besieged, plagued.

banes (line 6): evils.

A wilder beast from West (line 7): in 'The Wreck of the Deutschland', Hopkins called Luther the 'beast of the waste wood', because he was the author of the Reformation, which, to Hopkins, was heresy and disastrous schism. Here he is talking of a 'wilder beast' by which he means possibly the anti-religious liberal-rational kind of thinking growing in Europe, exemplified in Hopkins's mind by Swinburne and Hugo, 'those plagues of mankind' (*B*, 39). Possibly also he was thinking of Victorian materialism and industrialism which had degraded masses of humanity below animal level, creating bestiality and squalor. He talked of this in his letters and in his poems, e.g. 'The Loss of the Eurydice' where he talked of his 'Fast-foundering own generation', and 'The Sea and the Skylark' where he spoke of 'our sordid turbid time' and the sinking of humanity down to 'man's first slime'.

Her Perseus linger (line 9): a question, i.e. 'Will her Perseus linger?', etc.

leave her to her extremes (line 9): this and the following lines are prophetic of the religious soul in extremes of torment, which Hopkins himself was to undergo and which he expressed in the Sonnets of Desolation, notably in 'No worst, there is none'. The idea in the latter poem of a soul bound fast to a rock (or anvil), suffering violent pangs but seeking to be patient and even to rejoice in their midst, finds its germ here.

her patience . . ./Mounts (lines 12–13): in his 'Rules for the Discernment of Spirits', St Ignatius wrote:

Let him who is in desolation strive to remain in patience which is the virtue contrary to the troubles which harass him; and let him think that he will shortly be consoled.

(Rule VIII. *S*, 204)

The connection of the Andromeda story with the Church suffering and with the individual Christian soul in torment becomes increasingly obvious.

Gorgon's gear (line 14): Perseus was carrying the Gorgon's head which, even in death, was so frightful that it could turn men to stone. The legend relates that during his fight with the sea monster he laid it among the seaweed, which turned into coral.

barebill (line 14): sword.

thongs and fangs (line 14): i.e. the thongs that bound Andromeda and the fangs of the monster, both broken by Perseus. Hopkins is thinking of the Church eternally and mysteriously delivered from evil by Christ, even in the midst of its sufferings.

Metre: Hopkins wrote to Bridges, inviting 'minute criticism' on this poem, saying that he had attempted 'a more Miltonic plainness and severity' than hitherto. He added that he had not achieved either severity or plainness, but had at least avoided 'quaintness' (*B*, 87).

The poem is in standard rhythm, with a subtle counterpointing, set up by the overreaving of the lines into one another, and by the varying position of the pauses in each line. This, plus the alliteration, and vowel assonance and dissonance, gives a sinewy richness to the language.

Peace
(Oxford, 1879)

A first cry from the heart under the kind of suffering that was later to drive
him to the Sonnets of Desolation, this poem is sweetly muted in its contemplation of distress and strongly hopeful in the consolations of patience.
In it the poet asks Peace, here imaged as a 'wild wooddove, shy wings shut',
if she will ever come to roost in his heart. He admits honestly that he
would like to have peace, but has very little. In the second part he reflects
that at least God has given him patience to bear his unrest, and that patience
may finally lead to peace, not in the sense of passive bliss but in the sense of
the divine contemplation that leads to fruitful action. Here, as ever, Hopkins is thinking of his priestly vocation.

under be (line 2): like 'round me roaming' this is a typical Hopkins inversion in this case giving a liquid sweetness to the line. It also conveys a
sense of peace underlying his very being.

To own my heart (line 4): i.e. to my own heart. He is not going to pretend
that his heart does not long for peace.

piecemeal peace (line 5): sporadic peace. W. H. Gardner calls this line 'a
running logic of feeling mixed with sound' (*WHG*, Vol. II, 286).

What pure peace allows . . . ? (lines 5–6): an anguished question: 'What sort
of "pure" peace is it that allows noise of war and actual conflict which are
the things that annihilate peace?' Hopkins is of course referring to the
periodic pain and turbulence of his own inner life which afflicted him
throughout his adult life. See 'The Wreck of the Deutschland', sts. 1–3,
'The Caged Skylark', and the later Sonnets of Desolation. There are many
entries in his early Journal which testify likewise, e.g. *J*, 236, 238, 249–50.

the daunting wars, the death of it (line 6): an awkward phrase and a weak
ending to the line.

reaving Peace (line 7): 'Reave is for plunder, carry off' (*B*, 196). The sense
is: 'O surely since he takes away my peace, the Lord should leave me some
compensation'.

exquisite (line 8): a remarkable adjective, conveying both the smoothness of
self-mastery and the keen touch of pain.

That plumes to Peace (line 9): the sense is 'that leads to peace' but the verb
'plumes' suggests many things, e.g. leading or settling down to peace,
acquiring a covering of peace, flying heavenwards to peace hereafter. Also,
as W. H. Gardner suggests, the word can suggest renunciation, the strip-
ping a way of inessentials (*WHG*, Vol. II, 287). Cf. 'Patience, hard thing',

where the poet, using the same kind of imagery, tells of the enormous difficulty and of the rewards of patience.

brood and sit (line 11): at first this does not seem to agree with the idea of 'work to do' unless it is remembered that the dove is, biblically, the Spirit that brooded over the face of the waters and brought forth all creation. The only peace, therefore, which the soul of Hopkins the priest could enjoy would be the peace of contemplation from which is born the activity which brings about the New Creation in Christ. See his notes on 'Three Ways of Praying' (*S*, 208–9).

Metre: This poem, like 'Pied Beauty' is a curtal sonnet, i.e. a shortened form of sonnet—6 + 4½ instead of the usual 8 + 6 lines. The metre is 'standard Alexandrines', i.e. lines of six iambic feet. The length of the lines, the softly inwoven alliteration and the liquid vowel sounds are all powerfully evocative of the peace which the poet most desired.

At the Wedding March
(Bedford Leigh, Lancashire, 21 October 1879)

The title was originally 'At a Wedding'. The alteration pinpoints the priestly meditation at the climax of the ceremony, as bride and groom, newly wed, walk down the aisle away from the altar and out towards life.

The poem is the thoughts and prayers of the priest as he watches them go.

hang your head (line 1): i.e. as with a garland. Cf.
. . . she shall bring thee to honour when thou dost embrace her. She shall give to thine head an ornament of grace.
(Proverbs, iv, 8)
lissome (line 3): slim, graceful.
scions (line 3): Offspring.
deeper than divined (line 6): deeper than you ever guessed.
dear charity,/Fast you ever . . . bind (lines 7–8): a memory of St Paul's teaching in Colossians iii, where he speaks of the bond of charity (i.e. love) which makes all Christians 'one body' in Christ. To foster and strengthen this bond, which is the way towards human perfection and a pledge of Heaven, he urges husbands and wives to love one another.
I to him turn with tears (line 10): i.e. to Christ, who turned marriage into a sacrament—something started in time but finished in eternity—thus giving it 'immortal years'. The tears are tears of joy, also perhaps of solicitude, for Hopkins, in W. H. Gardner's words 'knew that Christian marriage is, among other things, a spiritual battlefield, on which merit may be won or lost' (*WHG*, Vol. II, 289).

Metre: sprung rhythm, 4 stresses per line; e.g.

/   /   /   /
With lissome scions, sweet scions.

Although this poem was written at Liverpool, where Hopkins was appointed in January 1880 to the large Jesuit Church of St Francis Xavier, the events described probably took place at Leigh, Lancashire, where he spent three months, September–December 1879.

This short stay was probably one of the happiest times of Hopkins's priesthood. He had not been particularly happy at Oxford, which might have been expected to suit him, and it is strange that he found fulfilment in a small and dreary town in the industrial wasteland of east Lancashire. '*in this smoke-sodden little town*', writes Father Devlin

... he came up against people who needed him desperately and their need was what he needed. A man must fall in love with his parish or cure of souls if he is to do well by it. Hopkins fell in love with Leigh as he had never quite been able to do, in spite of 'The Bugler Boy' and 'The Handsome Heart', with Oxford.
(Introduction to Hopkins's Sermons, *S*, 5)

The poem is a priestly meditation on the death of one of his parishioners, a burly blacksmith. Physical beef and brawn, and the rude health that accompanies it, had a fascination for the small, ailing and sensitive Hopkins, and here it gives him consolation to remember how his priestly care helped the blacksmith, shattered in health, to peace with God and a happy death.

farrier (line 1): a blacksmith. A flourishing trade in an industrial town where transport of heavy goods was effected by waggons pulled by teams of drayhorses.

till time when (line 3): i.e. till the time came when.

anointed and all (line 6): the 'and all' is a Lancashire colloquial tag. Compare 'all road ever' below, and the dialect, 'fettle'.

a heavenlier heart (line 6): a disposition more resigned (to God).

our sweet reprieve and ransom (line 7): Holy Communion. One view of Christ's suffering and death was that it was a kind of ransom-offering to God, by His own Son, who thus reprieved the human race from the sentence of death that lay upon it.

all road ever (line 8): in whatever way. Preaching at Bedford Leigh Hopkins had used the same Lancashire expression also in connection with sin:

There is a crowd of you, brethren, and amidst that crowd some must be

in this road—*I mean are out of your duty, out of God's grace, and in mortal sin.*
(*S*, 47)

child (line 11): in the spiritual sense.

How far from then forethought of, etc. (line 12): i.e. how far you were, then, in your boisterous years from forethought of sickness and death. A memorable line, elliptical, inverted yet crystal-clear. The last three lines of the poem are solemn and splendid in their rhetoric.

random grim forge (line 13): W. H. Gardner suggests that 'random' has an architectural meaning, 'built of stones of irregular sizes and shapes'. It also carries associations of 'unthinking', the careless days of a powerful man in his prime.

fettle (line 14): dialect, 'fix'.

Metre: The poem is in sprung rhythm, with six stresses per line and many outriding feet. W. H. Gardner in his *Study* gives a detailed scansion of the poem based on the careful collation of three texts (*WHG*, Vol. I, 102). He notes fifteen outriding feet:

1.1 *Randal . . . farrier . . . dead then?*

1.3 *Pining, pining . . . rambled in it.* 1.5 *broke him. Impatient*

1.8 *Tendered to him. Ah well* 1.9 *endears them.*

1.11 *child, Felix* 1.12 *forethought of* 1.13 *random grim forge*

1.14 *drayhorse*

Brothers
(Hampstead, August 1880)

Five varying drafts of this poem exist, carefully collated by Bridges to produce this version. Both Dixon and Bridges criticized it on various counts, and the modifications spread over two years 1879–81.

The original incident took place at Mount St Mary's College, Chester-field, Derbyshire, where Hopkins was sub-minister from October 1877 to May 1878. On 14 August 1879 he wrote from Oxford, to Bridges as follows:

I hope to enclose a little scene that touched me at Mount St Mary's. It is something in Wordsworth's manner; which is, I know, inimitable and un-approachable, still I shall be glad to know if you think it a success, for pathos has a point as precise as jest has and its happiness 'lies ever in the ear of him that hears, not in the mouth of him that makes'.

(*B*, 86)

A year later he told Bridges that he had written it in stanzas 'in Words-worth's manner' but when he had compared it with the latter's 'inimitable simplicity and gravity', he almost destroyed it. Instead he changed the metre 'which made it do' (*B*, 106).

It is an attempt to reproduce the simplicity of Wordsworth's *Lyrical Ballads* which took incidents from common life and reproduced them in 'the real language of men', at the same time capturing their deepest poignancy or significance. Hopkins is too unaccustomed to a homely style really to bring it off, but the narrative goes at a brisk pace and the last six lines serve to bring out the human significance of the episode.

Life all laced in the other's, Love-laced (lines 2–3): The original version was:

How lovely is the elder brother's
Love, all laced in the other's
Being . . .

(*D*, 44)

but Dixon objected to the couplet running on into the third line. So Hopkins altered it 'in deference to both yours and Bridges' criticisms' (*D*, 49).

Shrovetide (line 5): the time immediately before Lent when people came to be 'shriven' (Old English) or cleansed of their sins by confession.

By meanwhiles (line 15): from time to time.

lost in Jack (line 18): totally absorbed in his brother's forthcoming appearance on the stage.

diver's dip (line 20): Bridges must have objected, for some reason, to this phrase being near to 'lost in Jack' above. Hopkins could not see the force of the objection, and wrote: 'the one is a common metaphor . . the other is descriptive of a physical trick of restless impatience' (*B*, 119).

Truth's tokens tricks like these (line 22): the fourth edition reading is 'And many a mark like these'. The sense of both readings is that Henry's behaviour is a sign of deep and genuine feeling.

Nay, roguish ran the vein (line 28): i.e. of Jack's humour. Far from being nervous, he was mischievously at ease.

Eh, how all rung (line 33): This piece of chatty colloquialism in the earlier edition is now replaced in the fourth edition by 'There! the hall rung'.

Young dog, he did give tongue (line 34): restored in fourth edition to 'Dog, he did give tongue!' Bridges must have made somewhat heavy weather of this line, for we find Hopkins writing to him in jocular reproof: *First you misquote, then you insult me. I wrote 'Dog, he did give tongue', not what you call like Browning, 'Dog, did he give tongue?'. It means, so to say, 'And by George, sir, when the young dog opened his mouth at last he did make a noise and no mistake'.* (*B*, 111)

framed in fault (line 38): i.e. distorted by Original Sin. '. . . the world' wrote Hopkins, 'is a frame of things consistent with and founded on sin'.

there's salt (line 39): i.e. to close up your wounds. The thought of the natural kindness of which the human heart is capable, despite sin, is a great consolation.

Metre: sprung rhythm with three stresses per line. Writing to Bridges about the *four*-stress line as in 'Spring and Fall' (q.v.) Hopkins had testified to the care he took to see that if one line had a heavy ending the next must have an accentuated syllable right at the beginning. In the case of the three-stress line, as here, however, this principle does not matter 'for the heavy ending or falling cadence of one line does not interfere with the rising cadence of the next, as you may see' (*B*, 120).

Spring and Fall
(Lydiate, Lancashire, 7 September 1880)

Hopkins wrote this poem while at Liverpool (1879–81), a period in his life that blighted his spirit with squalor, depression and overwork. On 5 September 1880, two days before he composed this poem he wrote to Bridges: *I take up a languid pen to write to you, being down with diarrhoea and vomiting, brought on by yesterday's heat and the long hours in the confessional. Yesterday was in Liverpool the hottest day of the year.*
(*B*, 104)

In the same letter, after writing the poem, he wrote that it was 'a little piece composed since I began this letter, not founded on any real incident. I am not well satisfied with it' (*B*, 109).

He sent it to Dixon in 1881 saying that it was composed while walking from Lydiate near Liverpool and adding that it was to have some plainsong music put to it. He concluded feelingly: 'Liverpool is of all places the most museless. It is indeed a most unhappy and miserable spot' (*D*, 42).

Not surprisingly therefore this is a sad little poem, on human mortality. The child weeps at the fall of leaves in autumn. Later, says the poem, she will realize that she really mourns her own mortality of which the leaf-fall is a symbol. The poem is reminiscent of the 'shades of the prison-house' note of Wordsworth's Immortality Ode. It is even more reminiscent perhaps of the grey despair of Macbeth's cry: 'My way of life is fallen into the sere, the yellow leaf.'

Goldengrove (line 2): the place could be anywhere, but there are distinct associations of the fading away of Paradise. Leaves are gold in autumn.
unleaving (line 2): i.e. unleafing—leaves falling.
It will come to such sights colder (line 6): the heart, as it grows older, will be unmoved at such sights.
Though worlds of wanwood leafmeal lie (line 8): 'wanwood' suggests pale dead forests. 'Leafmeal' suggests piece by piece (or leaf by leaf) disintegration and decay. A deleted line in another version read 'Though forests low and leafmeal lie' but Hopkins must have changed it to this powerful and visionary line which suggests silent worlds of desolation.
and know why (line 9): the child, weeping over autumn leaves, is really mourning for human mortality. Later she will come to this sad knowledge. As he says in the next lines the real source of grief is the same in either case.
springs (line 11): both in the sense of well-spring and also of beginning.

Nor mouth had (line 12): the general sense is that the child has no proper words for, nor understanding of, its own grief. But its heart half-knows and its 'ghost' (spirit) has guessed. Cf. Pascal 'The heart has its reasons that reason knows not of'.

the blight man was born for (line 14): i.e. Original Sin (and death) of which Hopkins learned so much at first hand in the degradation of the industrial slums. Even at the time of writing, the 'blight' was eating his soul. 'But I could never write', he told Bridges:

time and spirits were wanting; one is so fagged, so harried and gallied up and down. And the drunkards go on drinking, the filthy, as the scripture says, are filthy still: human nature is so inveterate. Would that I had seen the last of it. (*B*, 110)

Metre: 'in my lyrics in sprung rhythm', wrote Hopkins to Bridges, 'I am strict in overreaving the lines when the measure has four feet, so that if one line has a heavy ending the next must have a sprung head (or begin with a falling cadence) as—

    ／   ／   ／
Margaret, are you grieving

 ／   ／   ／   ／   ／   ／   ／
Over Goldengrove (and not e.g. Concerning Goldengrove) *unleaving?*
(*B*, 120)

    By a 'sprung head' Hopkins meant an accentuated first syllable.

Inversnaid
(28 September 1881)

Writing to Baillie in 1887, towards the end of his life, Hopkins expressed a longing for the peace of the Scottish Highlands:
I could wish I were in the Highlands. I never had more than a glimpse of their skirts. I hurried from Glasgow one day to Loch Lomond. The day was dark and partly hid the lake, yet it did not altogether disfigure it but gave a pensive or solemn beauty which left a deep impression on me. I landed at Inversnaid . . . for a few hours.
(FL, 288)
   Writing to Bridges in 1879, two years before the composition of this poem, Hopkins said:
I have . . . something, if I cd. only seize it, on the decline of wild nature, beginning somehow like this—
O where is it, the wilderness,
The wildness of the wilderness?
Where is it, the wilderness?
and ending—
And wander in the wilderness;
In the weedy wilderness,
Wander in the wilderness.
(B, 73–4)
   This project was probably abandoned, but the wilderness motif probably came to fruition in this poem when Hopkins visited Inversnaid. The visit, as he notes, was a fleeting one, and the actual imagery and materials used in the poem seem to be drawn from a cluster of entries in his early Notebooks of 1865, as may be seen below. 1865 was the year when he wrote 'The Alchemist in the City', an early embodiment of the deep longing for solitude away from the haunts of men. We touch here a persistent strain in his being which rarely found any fulfilment, but which crops up throughout his life, in his writings.

burn (line 1): (Scots) Stream.
In coop and in comb (line 3): an entry in the Early Diaries of 1865 reads: 'Brush and comb (how vastly absurd it is) both apply to . . . water ribs'. 'Combing' is the ribbed, fanlike effect of swift running water striking a stone and flowing over it. Hopkins produced this ribbed effect in a drawing of 1868 entitled 'At the Baths of Rosenlaui' reproduced in *J*. 'Coop' is probably the opposite of 'comb', the convex effect of water rushing over a

H.C.—9

sunken stone. In an adjacent *J* entry to the above he wrote: 'Water rushing over a sunken stone and hollowing itself to rise again seems to be devoured by the wave before which it forces up' (*J*, 67).

fleece (line 3): cf. 'The Wreck of the Deutschland', st. 16, 'cobbled foam-fleece'.

windpuff-bonnet of fawn-froth (line 5): i.e. the windblown vapour that rises from a pool at the foot of a waterfall. Hopkins's early journals are full of close observation of such phenomena. This, for example, from a visit to Switzerland, July 1868:

The vapour which beats up from the impact of the falling water makes little feeder rills down the rocks and these catching and running in drops along the sharp ledges in the rock are shaken and delayed and chased along them and even cut off and blown upwards by the blast of the vapour as it rises.
(*J*, 177)

twindles (line 6): W. H. Gardner suggests that this is a 'portmanteau word, inscaping "twists", "twitches" and "dwindles" (Notes to Penguin edition; also notes to 3rd edition, Oxford University Press).

Degged (line 9): Lancashire dialect word, meaning sprinkled.

groins of the braes (line 10): hillsides.

Wiry heathpacks (line 11): clumps of heather.

flitches (line 11): clumps.

beadbonny ash (line 12): the phrase, and indeed the whole line, has the authentic ring of Scottish folk song. Cf. the rhythm of the Skye Boat Song. 'Beadbonny': a little obscure, though Hopkins once noted in the same part of the Early Diaries mentioned above 'Ash clusters like grapes' (*J*, 67).

What would the world be, etc. (line 13): in the same set of notes, the young Hopkins toyed with the idea of a poem, dealing with streams in a silent wilderness. It began:

A noise of falls I am possessed by
Of streams; and clouds like mesh'd and parted moss.
(*J*, 66)

In the same year he wrote in 'The Alchemist in the City':

Then sweetest seems the houseless shore
Then free and kind the wilderness.

The wilderness was a symbol of something necessary to his being, the contact with 'the dearest freshness deep down things', itself a symbol of the waters of the spirit which spring to life everlasting.

'As kingfishers catch fire, dragonflies draw flame'
(Probably 1881)

This is a Scotist poem, in the sense that it hymns the uniqueness of each created thing. Everything in the whole scale of creation strives, in its own way, to realize what Duns Scotus called its '*haecceitas*'—its identity or unique selfhood. In so far as it does this, it gives glory to God. 'All things', wrote Hopkins, 'therefore are charged with love, are charged with God and if we know how to touch them give off sparks and take fire, yield drops and flow, ring and tell of him' (Meditation [*c*. 1881 *S*, 195).

In lines 1–8 Hopkins develops the thought of each thing in inanimate nature striving to broadcast its own inner identity. In the final sestet he turns to man, 'more highly pitched, selved and distinctive than anything in the world', who alone has freedom of choice, and who alone therefore can *choose* (or refuse) to give glory to God. For man to refuse however is for him to fail to realize his own deepest and most personal destiny, because in order fully to realize 'what in God's eye he is' (i.e. to realize his *haecceitas*) a man must *freely* will to give God glory. 'The moment we do this', wrote Hopkins, 'we reach the end (purpose) of our being' (*S*, 240 [Editor's brackets]). Hence the praise, in this sonnet of the 'loveliness' of the just man, who freely does the will of God.

catch fire . . . draw flame (line 1): the flash of the sun on the wings of kingfisher and dragonfly. Cf. Tennyson: 'The lightning flash of insect and of bird' ('Enoch Arden', quoted by Hopkins in a letter to Baillie, *FL*, 217).

tumbled over rim in roundy wells (line 2): the whole phrase is adjectival to 'stones', the language thus 'inscaping' the whole situation at the moment of impact. 'Roundy' is an older and here pleasanter version of 'round'.

tucked (line 3): an obsolete form of 'plucked'.

Bow (line 4): clapper.

to fling out broad its name (line 4): to broadcast to the world its inner essence. Same meaning as 'rehearsal/Of own, of abrúpt self' in Purcell sonnet. See also note on 'sake' in this poem, p. 90.

lines 3–4: There is subtle vowel chime (vowelling off) in these lines, inscaping in language the sound of bells.

Deals out that being (line 6): same as 'to fling out broad its name'.

indoors each one dwells (line 6): i.e. (the particular essence that) inside each one dwells.

Selves—goes itself (line 7): according to Hopkins, following Scotus, it is the function of each thing, each 'nature', once created, to 'selve' or to become completely itself. 'It is a function of a nature, even if it should be the whole function, the naturing, the *selving* of that nature' (Commentary on 'The Principle or Foundation', *S*, 125).

for that I came (line 8): by its mere existence, each thing in inanimate nature gives glory to God:

They glorify God but they do not know it. *The birds sing to him, the thunder speaks of his terror, the lion is like his strength, the sea is like his greatness, the honey like his sweetness; they are something like him, they make him known, they tell of him, they give him glory.*

(Instruction on 'The Principle or Foundation', *S*, 239)

Hopkins added that this is unconscious or 'dull' glory, but it is a glory unceasingly given—'what they do *they always do*'.

justices (line 9): as the bell's sound broadcasts its inner essence and gives glory to God, so the actions of the just man ('justicing') reveal his innermost nature tuned to the will of God.

Keeps grace (line 10): keeps close to the will of God. 'That' refers to the keeping of grace. The line once read 'Keeps grace and that keeps all his goings graces'.

what in God's eye he is—/Christ (lines 11–12): the doctrine is St Paul's doctrine of the Mystical Body, with a Scotist emphasis. The sense is that Christ's body is made present in and through the bodies of those who do God's will. He is present in them and they in Him. For a full explanation see Father Devlin's notes in *S*, 286, and also the conclusion to Appendix II of the same volume.

Christ plays in ten thousand places (line 12): the word 'plays' expresses the total freedom of the just man's assent to the will of God, and the communion thus established. In a meditation of December 1881, on 'the grace of graces', a continued and unconstrained correspondence between man and Christ, Hopkins wrote,

It is as if a man said: That is Christ playing at me and me playing at Christ, only that it is no play but truth; that is Christ being me *and me being Christ.*

(*S*, 154—Hopkins's roman)

Lovely in limbs, etc. (lines 13–14): the loveliness is of the spirit arising from the just man's perfect self-offering to and correspondence with Christ. There is a memory, however, of a sermon given in 1879 at Bedford Leigh, on the actual physical loveliness of Christ, whom Scotus taught was the eldest-born and the first in beauty among men:

There met in Jesus Christ all things that can make man lovely and loveable. In his body he was most beautiful. This is known first by the tradition in the

Church that it was so and by holy writers agreeing to suit those words to him | Thou art beautiful in mould above the sons of men . . .

I leave it to you, brethren, then to picture him, in whom the fullness of the godhead dwelt bodily, in his bearing how majestic, how strong and yet how lovely and lissome in his limbs, in his look how earnest, grave but kind. (S, 35–6)

Metre: Sprung rhythm, five stresses per line.

Ribblesdale
(Stonyhurst, 1882)

Hopkins meant this as a companion poem to 'In the Valley of the Elwy'.
After his year of tertianship at Manresa House, Roehampton, Hopkins
was appointed, in September 1882, to Stonyhurst College, near Blackburn,
Lancashire, a large public school run by the Jesuits. He wrote to Bridges
about the impressive size of the place, and the amount of building activity
going on, adding:
*There are acres of flat roof, which, when the air is not thick, as unhappily
it mostly is, commands a noble view of this Lancashire landscape, Pendle
Hill, Ribblesdale, the fells, and all round, bleakish but solemn and beautiful.*
(*B*, 151)
The manuscripts of the poem have a Latin epigraph, from Romans, viii,
19–20. The *RSV*, somewhat more intelligible here than the *AV*, renders the
passage as follows:
*For the creation waits with eager longing for the revealing of the sons of
God; for the creation was subjected to futility not of its own will but by the
will of him who subjected it in hope; because the creation itself will be set
free from its bondage to decay and obtain the glorious liberty of the children
of God.*
(Rom., viii, 19–21)
St Paul here is contemplating a universe, including man, subjected to decay
and death, and awaiting a renewal and a deliverance at the hands of God
who can make all things new. Although St Paul concludes that the creation
will be set free, Hopkins's poem dwells on the darker side of the story—
that man and nature are in bondage to evil and destruction. Man especially,
the heir to all creation (Gen., i, 28), has gone so far in wrong paths that
he is laying waste his rich inheritance both here and hereafter.

Ribblesdale: the river Ribble, flowing east to west, passes through some
of the pleasanter parts of rural Lancashire. Joined by the Hodder and the
Calder not far from where Hopkins was living at the time, it finally
broadens out to an estuary at Preston.
leaves throng (line 1): ' I mean "throng" for an adjective as we use it here
in Lancashire' (*D*, 109)
louchèd (line 2): '"louched" is a coinage of mine and is to mean much
the same as *slouch*ed *slouch*ing' (ibid.).
Thou canst but only be, but dost that long (line 4): in his notes on St
Ignatius's 'The Principle or Foundation', Hopkins noted that the things

of nature, though devoid of consciousness, nevertheless give a kind of glory to God by the mere fact of their existence:

... they tell of him, they give him glory, but they do not know they do, they do not know him, they never can, they are brute things that only think of food or think of nothing. This then is poor praise, faint reverence, slight service, dull glory. Nevertheless what they can they always do.

(*S*, 239—Hopkins's roman)

Thou canst but be, etc. (line 5): he continues his direct address to the natural creation.

strong/Thy plea with him (lines 5–6): metaphorically speaking, the things of nature, being so perfectly what they are, have a strong 'plea' with the Creator. The implication, with Hopkins, is always that man, the one creature that can *choose* to give glory to God, in fact fails to do so, and has no such plea.

nay does now deal (line 6): creation of the Ribble valley (or of anything) is not an event that happened once and for all in the past, but is something that has to be continually sustained moment to moment. God is the Creator *and* the Sustainer of nature.

reel (line 7): wind. The Ribble pursues a leisurely and twisting course.

and o'er gives all to rack or wrong (line 8): a gloomy and emphatic climax to the octave, the explanation of which occupies the sestet.

And what is Earth's eye, etc. (line 9): only through the mind and tongue of man can the dumb earth give conscious glory to God:

Man was created. Like the rest then to praise, reverence, and serve God; to give him glory. He does so, even by his being, beyond all visible creatures ... But man can know God, can mean to give him glory.

(ibid.—Hopkins's roman)

See also note on 'Life's pride and cared-for crown' in 'The Sea and the Skylark', p. 65.

the heir (line 10): i.e. to creation, but also to his 'own selfbent', to a nature and disposition twisted and blinded by Original Sin. '... attitudes of mind', wrote Hopkins in December 1881, are so lasting, so like everlasting, because they are so nearly absolute' (*S*, 153). The only answer to man's 'selfbent' is the grace of God, investing the creature with new possibilities of action,

... clothing its old self for the moment with a gracious and consenting self. This shift is grace. For grace is any action, activity, on God's part by which, in creating or after creating, he carries the creature to or towards the end of its being, which is its self-sacrifice to God and its salvation.

(*S*, 154)

tied to his turn (line 11): totally at the mercy of his own distorted nature.

To thriftless reave (line 12): another memorable inversion of word order. 'Reave' = rob, plunder. Hopkins had written in other poems of the ugly rapacity of Victorian industrialism, his fast-foundering own generation,[1] blearing and smearing the earth[2] and draining itself towards the primordial slime whence it came.[3] Here he returns to the theme of mankind so bound. to its own fallen nature that it ruins a rich inheritance, here and hereafter. In his Notes on 'The Principle or Foundation' he wrote:

Are we God's orchard or his vineyard? we have yielded rotten fruit, sour grapes or none. Are we his cornfield sown? we have not come to ear or are mildewed in the ear. Are we his farm? it is a losing one to him. Are we his tenants? we have refused him rent.

(*S*, 240)

this bids wear (line 13): 'this' (i.e. man's blindness and rapacity) 'bids' the earth wear 'brows' of care. Less metaphorically, if the earth could register an expression at man's plundering, it would be one of deep anxiety and distress. The sorrow would be less at the extent of the damage done than at the spectacle of 'life's pride and cared-for crown' thus plunging to degradation and taking the whole creation with him.

Metre: Mainly standard rhythm, heavily counterpointed, but one or two sprung lines, e.g. 11. 10–11 where some of the feet have two unstressed syllables.

[1] *'The Loss of the Eurydice'*, st. 22.   [2] *'God's Grandeur'*.
[3] *'The Sea and the Skylark'*.

The Leaden Echo and the Golden Echo
(Final version dated Stonyhurst, 13 October 1882)

This poem was designed for Hopkins's unfinished drama 'St Winefred's Well'. He started it in October 1879, and continued it at Liverpool, from whence he wrote to Bridges in September 1880:

You shall see the Leaden Echo when finished. The reason, I suppose, why you feel it carry the reader along with it is that it is dramatic and meant to be popular. It is a song for St Winefred's maidens to sing.
(*B*, 106)

The well of St Winefred is at Holywell, North Wales, not far from St Beuno's, where Hopkins spent his happy novitiate years. St Winefred was the daughter of a seventh-century Welsh chieftain, and the niece of St Beuno who was her spiritual teacher. According to the legend, her head was cut from her body by the chieftain Caradoc as she fled from him in defence of her chastity. St Beuno, to whose chapel she was fleeing, restored her to life, and a well of healing miraculous water sprang from the place where her head had fallen. Hopkins planned his drama to centre round this episode, and this poem is a meditation, by the maid, on beauty—how quickly it succumbs to age and age's evils despite all attempts to preserve it (The Leaden Echo), and how it can only be preserved for all eternity by being sacrificed and given back to God (The Golden Echo).

It was one of Hopkins's favourites. 'I never did anything more musical', he wrote to Dixon in 1886 (*D*, 149). Indeed it achieves a rich, hypnotic word-music which immerses the reader (or better the hearer) in contemplation. The spell is effected by a complex of techniques—rhyme, incantation, vowel-chime, vowel-run, alliteration and *cynghanedd* (see Introduction, p. 18).

Hopkins said, somewhat naively, that the poem 'ought to sound like the thoughts of a good but lively girl' (*B*, 158), which draws from Father Devlin a reminder of Henry James's remark that a good and lively girl could reproduce the thoughts of a Guardsman after one glance through a mess-room window (*S*, 215). Father Devlin adds, more seriously:

These choruses represented in fact the perfect fusion of his spiritual sensuousness and his religious ideals; they were in the high tradition of the seventeenth-century refusal to let beauty and morality go different ways.
(ibid.)

The Leaden Echo

bow or brooch, etc. (line 1): This line cost Hopkins some trouble and uncertainty. He wrote to Bridges from Stonyhurst in November 1882:

I cannot satisfy myself about the first line. You must know that words like charm *and* enchantment *will not do: the thought is of beauty as of something that can be physically kept and lost and by physical things only, like keys; then the things must come from the* mundus muliebris;[1] *and thirdly they must not be markedly oldfashioned. You will see that this limits the choice of words very much indeed.*

(*B*, 161–2—Hopkins's roman)

The line as printed represents his final choice after some alterations.

rankèd wrinkles (line 3): i.e. 'ranks' of wrinkles.

And wisdom is early to despair (line 8): because the wise girl realizes, sooner than the foolish one, that beauty does not last long.

The Golden Echo

Spare (line 1): i.e. stop—wait a minute.

I have one (line 2): i.e. a way to keep back beauty.

Hush there (line 2): i.e. stop weeping (addressed to the Leaden Echo).

Not within the singeing of the strong sun (line 4): i.e. not an earthly way.

passes of us (line 8): i.e. passes swiftly away from us. The three phrases—'prized . . . passes', 'fresh . . . fast flying', 'sweet . . . swiftly away',—are in balance.

wimpled-water-dimpled (line 10): lit. 'dimpled like the wimpled water', a compound adjective to 'face'. Cf. the use of 'wimpled' in line 2 of 'Morning Midday and Evening Sacrifice'. The general effect is of the soft curving mobility of a youthful face.

fleece of beauty (line 11): in 1885, Hopkins wrote to Bridges explaining his use of 'fleeced' in St Winefred's Well: 'I mean the velvetiness of rose-leaves, flesh and other things, *duvet*' (*B*, 215—Hopkins's italics).

Never fleets more (line 12): the clause beginning 'Where whatever's prized', after a long series of items in apposition, finally gets its verb here.

fastened with tenderest truth | To its own best being (lines 12–13): Hopkins means that in God all things are found in their highest causes, i.e. in their finest essence. The rest of the poem is devoted to showing how beauty, when offered and sacrificed to God, is preserved in all its loveliness for ever.

Come then, your ways, etc. (line 14): addressed to youth; 'Bring along,

---

[1] *Latin = 'the world of women'.*

offer all your gifts of beauty, youth and love, and "deliver them" (to Christ)'.

beauty-in-the-ghost (line 18): spiritual beauty. Here, as elsewhere, youth is urged to give its 'innocent mind and Mayday' to God while it is 'worth consuming'.

God, beauty's self and beauty's giver (line 19): a thought older than Plato, echoed later by the famous words of St Augustine at the time of his crisis of conversion, 'Late have I loved thee, O most ancient Beauty, ever old yet ever new' (*Confessions*).

hair of the head, numbered (line 21): an echo of Matt., x, 30 'But the very hairs of your head are numbered. Fear ye not therefore . . .' (See also Luke, xii, 7.)

Nay, what we had lighthanded left, etc. (line 22): Hopkins had to explain this to Bridges:

'Nay, what we lighthanded' etc means 'Nay more: the seed that we so carelessly and freely flung into the dull furrow, and then forgot it, will have come to ear meantime' etc.

(*B*, 159)

At the back of this metaphor is Hopkins's whole thought about sacrifice, summed up in Christ's words:

Except a corn of wheat fall into the ground and die, it abideth alone; but if it die it bringeth forth much fruit. He that loveth his life shall lose it; and he that hateth his life in this world shall keep it unto life eternal.

(John, xii, 24–5)

hurling a heavyheaded hundredfold (line 24): the thought is that the things that we have voluntarily sacrificed to God 'this side' (in this life) blossom a hundredfold 'that side' (in the world to come). The metaphor is still that of a single grain that 'dies' and grows into a full ear or head of wheat. The 'hundredfold' is probably an echo of Christ's words to his apostles after the rich young man, unable to stop clinging to his worldly possessions, had gone away sorrowful:

And everyone that hath forsaken houses, or brethren, or sisters, or father or mother, or children or lands, for my name's sake, shall receive an hundredfold, and shall inherit everlasting life.

(Matt., xix, 29)

In the context of his own life, Hopkins applied his teaching rigorously to himself, in his determined rejection of the poetic fame which would have been such a consolation and encouragement to him. In 1881, while this poem was being written, there was a moving exchange of letters between him and Dixon, who wanted some of Hopkins's poems to be printed. 'Surely one vocation cannot destroy another,' Dixon pleaded, 'and such a

Society as yours will not remain ignorant that you have such gifts as have seldom been given by God to man' (*D*, 90). But Hopkins remained firm: *Now if you value what I write, if I do myself, much more does our Lord. And if he chooses to avail himself of what I leave at his disposal he can do so with a felicity and with a success which I could never command . . . This is my principle and this in the main has been my practice . . . when one mixes with the world and meets on every side its secret solicitations, to live by faith is harder, is very hard; nevertheless by God's help I shall always do so.*
(*D*, 93)

haggard at the heart (line 26): cf. 'the sodden-with-its-sorrowing heart' of stanza 27 of 'The Wreck of the Deutschland', the real reason for the nun's call to Christ.

care-coiled (line 26): coiled means both 'wrapped round' and also 'disturbed'.

so fagged, so fashed (line 26): reminiscent of a prose cadence of one of his Liverpool letters of 1880: 'one is so fagged, so harried, and gallied up and down' (*B*, 110).

fashed (line 26): (Scots dialect) bothered, anxious.

cogged (line 26): (archaic) deceived, cheated, self-deluded. Hopkins at the time was reading the Rev. W. Barnes's *Outline of English Speech Dialect*, a brave attempt to restore English to 'a sort of modern Anglo-Saxon' (*B*, 162). Hopkins greatly sympathized with such aims and thought Old English 'a vastly superior thing to what we have now' (ibid., 163).

Yonder (line 31): this being a dramatic piece, these words would presumably be said as the Chorus left the stage, looking heavenwards.

Metre: Bridges must have compared this piece to the rhythmic prose of Walt Whitman, a view which drew forth a long and detailed refutation from Hopkins in a letter which he called his 'deWhitmanizer'. He insisted that the piece was in sprung rhythm:
. . . that piece of mine is very highly wrought. The long lines are not rhythm run to seed: everything is weighed and timed in them. Wait till they have taken hold of your ear and you will find it so. No, but what it is like is the rhythm of Greek tragic choruses or of Pindar: which is pure sprung rhythm. And that has the same changes of cadence from point to point as this piece.
(*B*, 157)

He went on to compare it with 'Binsey Poplars', also a two-stanza poem 'in the same kind and vein'.

There is no doubt, however, that sprung rhythm is not the exact science

Hopkins would have liked it to be, because stress markings are very much a matter of individual pronunciation. He began to realize this himself, for on one MS. of this poem he wrote: 'I have marked the stronger stresses, but with the degree of stress so perpetually varying no marking is satisfactory. Do you think all had better be left to the reader?'

He wrote to Patmore in September 1883, admitting that metre is not an exact science, but depends on individual pronunciation:

I used to object to things which satisfied Bridges and we came to the conclusion that our own pronunciation, by which everyone instinctively judges, might be at the bottom of the matter.

(*FL*, 313)

However, he was quite justified in distinguishing his choruses from the rhythmic prose of Whitman. The sway and incantation of the verse of Greek chorus is quite marked, as it is in a later imitation of these rhythms, the Choruses of T. S. Eliot's *Murder in the Cathedral*. Indeed, lines like

'Tall sun's tingeing, or treacherous the tainting of the earth's air'

immediately call Eliot's work to mind, since the inspiration springs from the same root in ancient Greek drama.

The Blessed Virgin Compared to the Air We Breathe
(Stonyhurst, May 1883)

Like 'The May Magnificat', this poem is a 'Maypiece'. In June 1883, Hopkins wrote to Dixon:

During May I was asked to write something in honour of the Blessed Virgin, it being the custom to hand up verse compositions 'in the tongues' (which sometimes are far fetched, for people gravitate to us from odd quarters): I did a piece in the same metre as 'Blue in the Mists all day', but I have not leisure to copy it.
(*D*, 108)

As with his previous Maypiece, Hopkins did not like this poem. 'It is partly a compromise with popular taste', he wrote to Bridges, 'and it is too true that the highest subjects are not those on which it is easy to reach one's highest' (*B*, 179).

Bridges, however, thought it admirable, and Coventry Patmore, whom Hopkins met about this time, though failing to understand most of the latter's work, also expressed 'high admiration' (*B*, 192).

'In this poem', writes W. H. Gardner in his notes to the third edition of Hopkins's poems,

G.M.H. says that just as the atmosphere sustains the life of man and tempers the power of the sun's radiation, so the immaculate nature of Mary is the softening, humanizing medium of God's glory, justice and grace. Through her the ineffable Godhead becomes comprehensible—sweetly attuneable to the limited human heart.
(op. cit., p. 241)

It is, in fact a 'metaphysical' poem in a great tradition—a prolonged analogy, lovingly worked out between apparently unrelated elements of experience, the air which surrounds, protects and nurtures our physical existence, and the spiritual ambience of the Blessed Virgin which gently fosters and protects our spiritual lives.

In the tender devotional tone, one is reminded of some of the seventeenth-century Metaphysical poets; of George Herbert, for instance, whose characteristic note is the quaint deep simplicity seen here in such couplets as,

My more than meat and drink,
My meal at every wink.

In at least one passage, however, in this poem by Hopkins—

Whereas did air not make
This bath of blue and slake

His fire, the sun would shake,
A blear and blinding ball
With blackness bound, and all
The thick stars round him roll
Flashing like flecks of coal,
Quartz-fret, or sparks of salt,
In grimy vasty vault.

—one is reminded of the mixed quaintness and imaginative splendour of Andrew Marvell, or even of the younger Milton.

That each eyelash or hair/Girdles (lines 3–4): i.e. that surrounds each eyelash or hair.

frailest-flixed (line 5): In a Journal entry of 1869, Hopkins noted a large cloud 'with a high blown crest of flix or fleece about it' (*J*, 192). 'Flixed' will here refer, therefore, to the feathery meshed softness of the snowflake.

riddles (line 7): permeates.

Now but to breathe its praise (line 15): even to speak in praise of it.

But mothers each new grace (line 22): i.e. is mother to each new grace, etc. At Bedford Leigh, Hopkins in a sermon, touched upon the subject of Mary as Mediatrix of all Graces:

Now holiness God promotes by giving grace; the grace he gives not direct but as if stooping and drawing it from her vessel, taking it down from her storehouse and cupboard. It is in some way laid up in her.

(*S*, 29–30. See also note on 'and no way but so', line 33)

Mary Immaculate (line 24): the dogma of the Immaculate Conception of Mary was solemnly proclaimed by Pope Pius IX in 1854. Hopkins explained it as follows, in a sermon at Bedford Leigh commemorating the twenty-fifth anniversary of the declaration:

... that the Blessed Virgin Mary was never in original sin; that unlike all other men and women, children of Adam, she never, even for one moment of her being, was by God held guilty of the Fall ... All others but Mary, even the holiest, have fallen at least in Adam ... her privilege has been granted to none but her.

(*S*, 43)

yet/Whose presence, power, etc. (lines 25–6): i.e. yet whose presence (and whose) power, etc. Popular Marian devotion in the Litanies calls Mary, 'Queen of Heaven', identifying her with the Woman of The Song of Solomon vi, 10, 'fair as the moon, clear as the sun and terrible as an army with banners', a conception which reappears on a cosmic scale in the Woman of Revelation, xii, 1, 'clothed with the sun and the moon under her feet, and upon her head a crown of twelve stars'.

and no way but so (line 33): the doctrine that God mediates all his graces to mankind exclusively through Mary has had a semi-canonical status in the Roman Catholic Church, though it is now being re-examined in the light of past tendencies to exaggeration and Mariolatry. It found its highest expression in the work of St Bernard, a leading figure in twelfth-century monasticism.

the same/Is Mary, more by name (lines 36–7): Mary *is* mercy. Cf. 'The sweet alms' self is her', line 43 below.

ghostly good (line 48): spiritual well-being. Hopkins always preferred the short Anglo-Saxon word 'ghost' to the Latin 'spirit'. On Mary's spiritual motherhood, he wrote that she is 'with great birthpangs the mother of all men in the spirit' (*S*, 170).

Laying (line 51): allaying and calming.

The deathdance in his blood (line 52): the image is simple, vivid and medieval, characteristic of one strain of Hopkins's personal faith. 'All men', he wrote, '. . . are by original sin lost as soon as conceived and we are here to consider the crying need for redemption' (ibid.).

And makes . . ./New Nazareths in us, etc. (lines 59–60): a mystical idea, at the same time perfectly practical. The whole point of Ignatian meditation with its use of all the powers of imagination is to recreate, here and now, any Biblical scene, and then to draw out its spiritual meaning. Thus, new Nazareths and new Bethlehems, the places of Christ's conception and birth, are constantly recreated in the soul of the spiritual man. Hopkins wrote very full notes on the Ignatian way of meditation in a projected Commentary on the Spiritual Exercises.

Men here may draw like breath (line 66): i.e. men, by contemplating the 'mysteries' or scenes of the Gospel may draw in the breath of eternal life in Christ as they at present draw in the natural breath of life in the air.

Who, born so, comes to be/New self, etc. (lines 68–9): Christ is born again in the soul of the believer who thus receives a 'new self'. Hopkins wrote of this spiritual transformation as 'a lifting him from one self to another self, which is a most marvellous display of divine power'. ('On Personaltiy Grace and Freewill', *S*, 151). Cf. also lines 12–14 of 'As kingfishers catch fire'.

Again, look overhead, etc. (line 73 etc.): the next 17 lines are devoted to an analogy which originated in a Bedford Leigh sermon of October 1879:

St Bernard's saying, All grace given through Mary: this is a mystery. Like blue sky, which for all its richness of colour does not stain the sunlight, though smoke and red clouds do, so God's graces come to us unchanged but all through her. Moreover she gladdens the Catholic's heaven and when she is brightest so is the sun her son.

(*S*, 29)

air is azurèd (line 74): i.e. steeped in blue which is, traditionally, Mary's colour.

sapphire-shot, etc. (line 79): shot-through, charged with and steeped in deep blue.

Or if there does some soft, etc. (lines 90–3): the general sense is that if this blue atmosphere which surrounds the world does alter the look of things it is to enhance their beauty.

Whereas did air not make, etc. (lines 94–102): Hopkins goes on, in this visionary passage, to describe what the universe would look like if the earth were not surrounded by this 'bath of blue' which 'slakes' the blinding ferocity of the sun.

So God was god of old (line 103): i.e. God appeared in Old Testament times as blinding and awful, until he appeared in a tender human way born of a woman.

our daystar (line 106): i.e. Christ. (Cf. Luke, i, 78); 2 Pet., i, 19). Mary gave him human flesh and limbs and so mediated God to the human race in a bearable way that would win our love.

isled (line 125): enfolded, as the sea enfolds an island.

Metre: Same metre as 'Brothers' (q.v.). It may be remarked that this metre is the English equivalent of the trimeter couplets in which some of the Latin hymns of the Church are composed.

No date is attached to this poem, but since it first appears in a collection of Hopkins's miscellaneous notes later entitled 'The Dublin Notebook', Humphry House concludes that it cannot be earlier than 1885 (*N*, 425).

A Sibyl was a prophetess endowed with visionary power, interpreting the will of the gods to men via the signs and portents of nature. Her message might be delivered in cryptic and mysterious fashion, in signs and parables requiring interpretation.

In this sombre and sinister poem, Hopkins spells out a message of God's doom and irrevocable judgment from the evening, as it slowly but inexorably covers the daylight world first with dusk, then with darkness, culminating in the emergence of the majestic constellations which 'overbend' the world with fiery radiance. Things are then seen, not as they appeared by day, but in simple black or white, which is a parable of the way things will appear on Judgment Day. The poem ends with the grim warning, redolent of the *Dies Irae*, of the fate of the soul which has chosen wrongly.

W. H. Gardner suggests that Hopkins may have had in mind the sixth book of Virgil's *Aeneid* when the Sibyl introduces the poet to the dark underworld. The beginning of the journey is in a bleak dim light when everything is stripped of colour, and the journey proceeds in a cavernous gloom similar to the atmosphere created in Hopkins's poem, in which evening itself appears as an immense vault encompassing birth, life and death.

It is a most impressive sonnet both in its sombre weight of atmosphere and in its length of line. 'I have at last completed but not quite finished the longest sonnet ever made and no doubt the longest making,' wrote Hopkins to Bridges in November 1886. 'It is in 8 foot lines and essays effects almost musical' (*B*, 245). It embodies Hopkins's highest technical skill in matters of assonance, alliteration and patterns of vowel-sound; in short the *cynghanedd* he learned in Wales.

It also incorporates, doubtless unconsciously, many of his memories, as may be seen below from the number of echoes of Journal entries of up to twenty years previous. His Journal itself was a careful recording and 'installing' of his sense impressions, and it is no longer any mystery that such memories may re-emerge, modified and blended, in later compositions.

Earnest, earthless, etc. (line 1): this first line is a carefully 'lettered', slow incantation of adjectives to 'evening', which occurs in the next line. The exact logical sense of each word is secondary to the total atmosphere produced by the whole line, but the following meanings may be suggested: 'Earnest' because of the sense of silent inexorable purpose; 'earthless' because of the unearthly and luminous silence; 'equal' because evening softens, mutes and merges the hard realities of day; and 'attuneable' because it attunes the soul of man to mystery. The words 'vaulty, voluminous' suggest cavernous space and a dim light. There is a pause and the whispered 'stupendous' (now spoilt by twentieth-century over-use) leads on to the next line.

Evening strains (line 2): i.e. moves on towards its purpose. One evening in 1870 Hopkins, having seen the northern lights and the movement of the stars wrote,

This busy working of nature wholly independent of the earth and seeming to go on in a strain *of time not reckoned by our reckoning of days and years but simpler and as if correcting the preoccupation of the world by being* preoccupied with and appealing to and dated to the day of judgment *was like a new witness to God and* filled me with delightful fear.

(*J*, 200 Editor's roman)

The main themes of this poem can here be seen coming together in his mind fifteen years earlier.

womb-of-all, home-of-all, hearse-of-all night (line 2): birth, life and death, a progression of ideas linked by assonance and deliberately jarred at the end by the surprising and dissonant 'hearse'.

Her fond yellow hornlight, etc. (line 3): a hypnotic vowel-run, produced by a careful 'lettering' of the syllables, i.e. by a careful organization of assonance, vowel-change and alliteration. The precise meaning of 'hornlight' and 'hoarlight' is a matter of some debate. Dr Leavis suggests the former is soft moonlight, and the latter cold starlight (in *New Bearings in English Poetry,* Chatto [London, revised ed., 1950]). From internal evidence, however, such as a Journal entry noting 'horny rays the sun makes behind a cloud' (*J*, 200) and another noting 'spokes of dusty gold' at sunset (*J*, 234), the 'hornlight' would be the rays of the setting sun. In any case 'wound' here means 'is wound', i.e. a process already completed, which would rule out moonlight.

fond (line 3): because of the gentle softness of the yellow. 'Sundown yellow, moist with light', Hopkins once noted in his Journal (*J*, 196), and in a later entry he remarked, 'Bright sunset . . . westward lamping with tipsy bufflight the colour of yellow roses' (*J*, 236). The word 'wound' has other, more distant associations—e.g. of far-off 'horns' or trumpets in the west, heralding judgment.

wild hollow hoarlight (line 3): Hopkins in 1884 had contributed to the correspondence in the journal *Nature* on the remarkable sunsets which occurred all over the world as a result of light reflected off volcanic dust thrown into the upper atmosphere in the colossal eruption of the volcano Krakatoa in 1883. He noted strange afterglows 'high up in the sky, sometimes in the zenith', *after* sunset. He remarked on the nature of the glow 'which is both intense and lustreless'—'it bathes the whole sky, it is mistaken for the reflection of a great fire . . . more like inflamed flesh than the lucid reds of ordinary sunsets' (Printed in Appendix II, *D*, 163–4). Memories of this bleak strange light remaining in the zenith have obviously entered this poem.

earliest stars, earlstars, stars principal (line 4): once again a threefold progression in time, enfolding a daring play on words. The sky gradually fills with stars ('earliest stars, earlstars') till finally the great constellations ('stars principal') appear 'overbending' the earth as if judging it, and outlining in radiance ('fire-featuring') the face of heaven. This line continues the sense of superhuman movement and purpose suggested in line 2.

earth her being has unbound (line 5): the 'being' of the earth, to the Scotist Hopkins, consisted in her endless variety of colour and shape and 'self'. This 'dapple' (variety and contrast—see 'Pied Beauty') becoming merged and blurred at night, a complete loss follows of the 'selfhood' of each thing.

throughther (line 6): i.e. through each other, suggesting a dissolution of sharp inscape into formless chaos. Bridges quotes Burns's 'Halloween': 'They roar an' cry a' throughther' (Notes to 1st edition, p. 111).

pashed (line 6): disintegrated into a formless mass.

Disremembering (line 7): an Irish word, suggesting the psychic equivalent of physical dismembering. The sound of the word suggests a soft sinking into oblivion. Hopkins had used its opposite 'membering' to describe the distinctiveness of natural things:

What I most noticed was the great richness of the membering of the green in the elms, never however to be expressed but by drawing after study.
(*J*, 153)

Heart, you round me right (line 7): 'round'—to warn, to whisper. He listens to a voice from his heart.

Our evening is over us (line 8): his heart speaks, warning of the inevitability of death.

beakleaved boughs dragonish (line 9): 'beak-leaved' because sharply silhouetted against the light. The words convey the sinister and eerie quality of the scene.

damask the tool-smooth bleak light (line 9): to damask is to inlay an intricate pattern, as on a damascened sword. An entry in the Journal for 26–27

September 1873 shows Hopkins associating leaves against light with silver-work and fine craftsmanship;

Almost no colour; the cedar laying level crow-feather strokes of boughs, with fine wave and dedication in them, against the light . . .

. . . printed on the sun, a glowing silver piece, came out the sharp visible leafage of invisible trees, on either side nothing whatever could be seen of them.

(*J*, 239)

Our tale, O our oracle (line 10): an exclamation, 'O what a parable is here for humanity'. The explanation follows that no matter how varied ('skeined stained veined') the thread of life has been, it must resolve itself in the end on 'two spools' of moral good and evil, just as the leaves have in the end come to a simple black upon white.

Hopkins, despite his love of the colour and variety of life, had always seen life in this uncompromising way—perhaps too much so because, as Father Devlin points out, it savours more of bleak Kantian moralism than of wise spirituality.

part, pen, pack (line 11): i.e. let life part, pen, pack, etc. He abandons the metaphor from spinning and takes up the Biblical one of sheep and goats.

reckon but, reck but, mind/But (lines 12–13): the heart continues its warning in the triple manner characteristic of this poem.

'These two' refers to 'black, white; right, wrong'.

ware of a world, etc. (line 13): i.e. beware of the life to come, when only these two things count. The extreme lengths to which Hopkins was pre-pared to go, in his fine balancing of bliss and damnation, is illustrated by an 1868 letter to the Rev. E. W. Urquhart, an Anglican clergyman, thinking of 'going over to Rome', but hesitating. Hopkins urges the dire conse-quences of hesitation:

The difference between a state of grace and a state of reprobation, that differ-ence to wh. all other differences of humanity are as the splitting of straws, makes no change in the outer world; faces, streets and sunlight look just the same: it is therefore the more dangerous and terrible. And if God says that without faith it is impossible to please Him and will not excuse the best of heathens . . . what is to be said of people who knowing it live in avowed doubt whether they are in His church or not? Will it comfort you at death not to have despaired of the English Church if by not despairing of it you are out of the Catholic Church?

(*FL*, 51–2)

The passing of the years never abated the basic rigour of Hopkins's views—Puritan Englishman and Ultramontane Catholic at the same time.

of a rack/Where, selfwrung, selfstrung, etc. (lines 13–14); a vision of Hell which basically is eternal isolation from God with nothing to experience save oneself. In an interesting meditation upon the pain and isolation of the damned, Hopkins wrote:

... after death the soul is left to its own resources, with only the scapes and species *of its past life; which being unsupplemented or undisplaced by a fresh continual current of experience, absorb and press upon its consciousness.* (*S*, 139)

In the case of the blessed, this pressure turns to bliss, but in the case of the damned it turns to torment sweeping the sinner 'to an infinite distance from God; and the stress and strain of his removal is his eternity of punishment' (ibid.). See also notes on the concluding lines of 'I wake and feel the fell of dark'.

Metre: sprung rhythm with 8 feet in each line. The first line has a 'rest' of one foot. Of this poem, Hopkins wrote:

Of this long sonnet above all remember what applies to all my verse, that it is, as living art should be, made for performance and that its performance is not reading with the eye but loud, leisurely, poetical (not rhetorical) recitation, with long rests, long dwells on the rhyme and other marked syllables and so on. This sonnet shd. be almost sung: it is most carefully timed in tempo rubato.
(*B*, 246)

To What Serves Mortal Beauty?
(23 August 1885)

Bridges had to make a final choice from a number of slightly varying versions of this poem; two in his own possession, a copy sent by Hopkins to Canon Dixon, and an original draft found in the poet's posthumous papers. The main guide is the version sent to Dixon.

The poem asks and answers a question: 'What is the purpose of human physical beauty?' Beauty can be 'dangerous' because it arouses passion and it can flaunt itself in pride. Nevertheless it can be a source of great good, as when Pope Gregory, noticing the beauty of two captured British boys in the Roman slave market, sent his emissary Augustine to evangelize Britain. We should try to love people for their inner beauty of character and, as far as physical beauty is concerned, we should acknowledge it as Heaven's gift but not allow ourselves to be swayed by it when we meet it.

dangerous (line 1): because the sight of physical beauty tends to arouse the passions which are, traditionally, distractions from the spiritual life. Monastic enclosure, and the old religious practice of 'custody of the eyes', were in part designed to avoid such distraction. Hopkins wrote to Bridges on this topic of beauty, as follows:
I think then no one can admire beauty of the body more than I do, and it is of course a comfort to find beauty in a friend or a friend in beauty. But this kind of beauty is dangerous. Then comes the beauty of the mind, such as genius, and this is greater than beauty of the body and not to call dangerous. (*B*, 95)
He went on in the same letter to talk of the highest kind of beauty, beauty of character or the 'handsome heart', a theme which he dwelt on in the poem of this name, and to which he returns briefly here in line 10.
The O-seal-that-so feature (line 2): i.e. the kind face or form that would make an artist wish to perpetuate it. A first draft version was 'face feature-perfect'.
flung prouder form | Than Purcell tune lets tread to (lines 2–3): Hopkins had written in the Purcell sonnet (q.v.) of the utter individuality of Purcell's music, 'the rehearsal/Of own, of abrúpt sélf'. Purcell's music was, however, perfectly himself. Here, in the case of beauty, there is a 'flung prouder form', a tendency towards a self-conscious exhibitionism, of which Purcell was never guilty.
keeps warm | Men's wits to the things that are (lines 3–4): i.e. keeps men vividly aware of the (spiritual) reality of things. '. . . even bodily beauty', wrote

Hopkins, 'even the beauty of blooming health, is from the soul' (*B*, 95).

Master more may (line 5): may effect more.

How then should Gregory (line 7): an example of how a glance has affected history. The story is that Pope Gregory (*c.* A.D. 600) saw some fair-haired, blue-eyed British boys, 'windfalls of war's storm', on the Roman slave market. Moved by their beauty of feature, he exclaimed '*Non Angli sed angeli*' (not English but rather angels), and sent Augustine, later St Augustine of Canterbury, to Christianize England. This was 'that day's dear chance' dealt by God to a nation, through mortal beauty.

swarmed Rome (lines 7–8): replaced an earlier 'thronged Rome'.

Our law (line 10): possibly the Christian code, all men being worthy of love because made in the image of God.

Self flashes off frame and face (line 11): Hopkins seems to be saying that what a man *is* can be gathered from his facial expression and physical appearance.

Merely meet it (line 12): i.e. 'Meet it and do nothing more—do not be drawn into desire and passion'. Should be read with an emphasis on 'Merely'.

own,/Home at heart, etc. (lines 12–13): acknowledge it, in your heart, to be a gift of heaven.

Yea, wish that though, wish all, etc. (line 14): i.e. 'but wish for that beautiful person, and indeed for all people, a better kind of beauty, the grace of God'.

Metre: Standard rhythm, highly stressed, alexandrines (i.e. 6 stresses per line). Hopkins sent a copy to Dixon with a note: 'the mark ⌐———¬ over two neighbouring syllables means that, though one has and the other has not the metrical stress, in the recitation stress they are to be about equal' (*D*, 129). He marked thus the following syllables:

1.1 *To what serves*

1.3 *See: it does this: keeps warm*

1.4 *Men's wits to the things that are*

1.5 *Master more may than gaze*

1.6 *windfalls of war's storm*

1.10 *what are love's worthiest*

1.11 *World's loveliest—men's selves*

1.12 *What do then? how meet beauty?*

1.13 *then leave, let that alone*
(*D*, 129)
(The symbol ⌢ = elision or running of one syllable quickly into another.)

(*The Soldier*)
(Clongowes, August 1885)

The poem was found, along with 'Carrion Comfort' and 'Mortal Beauty' on a single sheet in Hopkins's posthumous papers. Bridges supplied the title, hence the brackets.

The poem, like 'To What Serves Mortal Beauty?' poses a question. Why do we bless a soldier when we see one? The answer is because his calling is a fine and manly one, and in our hearts we wish to credit the man with the valour and dedication his uniform represents.

In the sestet, the poet, as befits a follower of St Ignatius, links the topic to Christ, who, in his way, was a soldier, serving a cause to the end and giving his all. When Christ, now in Heaven, spies someone giving himself to the last gasp he 'leans forth' and blesses that man as a worthy follower of his.

The application to the poet himself is plain enough. All his working life, despite weakness and melancholy, he never swerved from his valorous strivings 'to do all that man can do' in the soldier-service of his Lord.

Yes. Why do we all, etc. (line 1): he takes up the theme as if he had already been discussing it with himself or another.

seeing of a soldier (line 1): the 'of' is probably a Victorian working-class colloquialism, such as Hopkins occasionally permitted himself. See, for example, 'Brothers' and 'Felix Randal'.

redcoats (line 2): British soldiers used to be dressed in red.

tars (line 2): sailors. The traditional, but now long-obsolete image of the British sailor was of Jolly Jack Tar, with pigtail, straw hat and bell-bottomed trousers. Even at this date, Hopkins's expression would be a trifle old-fashioned.

nay but foul clay (line 3): Hopkins had been chaplain to a barracks at Oxford earlier in his career, and would be under no illusions about military men.

Here it is (line 3): i.e. the answer to the question.

the heart,/Since, proud, it calls, etc. (lines 3–5): the syntax of these lines is: 'Since the heart calls the soldier's vocation proud and manly, it guesses, hopes and makes believe that the men who follow it also have these qualities personally.'

dears (line 6): i.e. values. The heart values the artist after the kind of work he produces. The first draft of this line was 'It fancies; it deems; dears the artist after his art'.

as sterling as all is smart (line 7): the heart would wish to find the soldier's inner character as fine as his outward appearance.

And scarlet wear (line 8): i.e. the heart would fain share the valorous spirit expressed in the scarlet uniform.

Mark Christ our King (line 9): The Ignatian Exercises, obligatory for Jesuits, picture Christ as a great king, out to conquer the earth, and to put Satan's legions to flight. This background would be very strongly in Hopkins's mind, as a potent conviction, not just as a fanciful metaphor. One meditation, 'The Two Standards', sets the composition of place as follows:

... to see a vast plain embracing the whole region round Jerusalem where the supreme Captain-General of the good is Christ our Lord; and another plain in the region of Babylon, where the chief of the enemy is Lucifer.

(Text printed in *S*, 178)

The aim of another meditation, 'Christ the King' is,

... to see Christ our Lord, the eternal King, and before him the whole of mankind, all of whom and each one in particular he calls saying: 'My will is to conquer the whole world and all my enemies, and so to enter into the glory of my Father. Whosoever, therefore, desires to come with me must labour with me in order that following me in suffering, he may likewise follow me in glory.'

(ibid., 160)

reeve a rope (line 10): Hopkins misspelt the word 'reave' in the MS. Bridges, thinking that he had also mistaken the meaning of the word, substituted the awkward word 'handle'. W. H. Gardner, editing the third edition, restored 'reeve' an old word meaning to thrust through, to tie or to twist. Hopkins used it here for the alliterative effect as much as for the precise meaning.

There he bides in bliss (line 10): a quaint medieval phrase, as is the image in the next line of Christ leaning forth from Heaven. The doctrine behind it is that the Humanity of Christ exists bodily in Heaven.

all that man can do (line 11): an ideal reflected in the Ignatian prayer, which asks only

To give and not to count the cost
To fight and not to heed the wounds
To toil and not to seek for rest
To labour and not to ask for any reward
Save knowing I do thy will.

So God-made-flesh does too (line 13): i.e. does all that man can do. Hopkins was fond of meditating on Philippians, ii, 7–8, the text about the total self-emptying of Christ who, although God, became fully man and went through all that man can suffer, even as far as a humiliating death on a cross.

'it should be this' (line 14): i.e. as a soldier, or at least as one ready to give everything, even life.

Metre: similar to that of 'To What Serves Mortal Beauty?', a highly stressed sonnet, i.e. with some 'unofficial' stresses in addition to the basic six per line. For example, W. H. Gardner writes about line 6:

R.B.'s note, *'fancies, feigns, deems,* takes three stresses', will not stand; we must read:/*It fáncies, feigns, deems, déars,*/or else give a half-stress to *deems,* in order to preserve the six-stress pattern.

(Notes to 3rd edition, p. 244)

The sonnets to which the following remarks apply are:
(Carrion Comfort) (p. 149)
'No worst, there is none' (p. 152).
'I wake and feel the fell of dark, not day' (p. 158)
'Patience, hard thing!' (p. 161)
'My own heart let me more have pity on' (p. 163)
'Thou art indeed just, Lord, if I contend' (p. 178)

They are all masterpieces, wrung out of despair and aridity, 'chronicles of
the Lord's suffering servant parched and bare'. Most of them were written
in 1885 during and after a long bout of psychological torment which
crushed Hopkins nearly to madness. At times he barely believed himself
out of Hell, and clung with mere intellect to the theological distinction
between the fires and rackings of the damned and the human agony of his
'sweating self' encased in the pains of desolation.

The attacks were nothing new. The bout that produced most of the
sonnets was particularly long and severe, but he had felt this way before,
and he knew he would again—'hours I mean years, mean life'.

The causes were hardly to be found in his outward circumstances which,
after he went to Ireland, were easy enough, apart from the drudgery of
marking large quantities of examination scripts. He was admittedly a
patriotic Englishman, in an Ireland seething with Home Rule unrest, and
found himself dragged unwillingly in the wake of Irish Jesuit enthusiasm:
*... greatly given over to a partly unlawful cause, promoted by partly unlawful
means, and against my will my pains, laborious and distasteful, like prisoners
made to serve the enemies' gunners, go to help on this cause.*
(*S*, 262)
But these factors were not the prime causes of the rending despair of the
sonnets.

Years of frustration have gone into these poems—half a working lifetime when he had done nothing but 'do without, take tosses, and obey'.
He was a gifted preacher who did not make the grade, probably because
of certain eccentricities, a scholar who produced no major work, a lover
of beauty who spent years in the most soul-killing industrial slums, a poet
who received no recognition, and a priest whose talents, perhaps because
of their variety, never found full employment. Above all he lacked even
an average vitality and good spirits which can make life tolerable. 'The
body cannot rest', he wrote,

... when it is in pain nor the mind be at peace as long as something bitter distils in it, and it aches. This may be at any time and is at many: how then can it be pretended there is for those who feel this anything worth calling happiness in this world.
(*S*, 262)

Finally, however, one must look deeper still for the root cause: into the deep, stubborn, harsh wilfulness which made Hopkins force, bend and drag his nature into what he deemed to be the highest service, of God. He was an imperialist in politics and also in his attitude towards the weaker and recalcitrant elements of his own nature. Perhaps because of his ingrained English puritanism he forgot, most of the time, the dictum of St Thomas Aquinas that grace is built upon nature, not upon the abolition of nature.

Right from early days one can see this destructive ruthlessness with himself. C. N. Luxmoore, writing to Arthur Hopkins in 1890 after the poet's death, records that Gerard at school abstained from all liquids for three weeks to prove some argument about the endurance of seamen. Just before the end, Gerard showed his tongue to some of the bigger boys— it was black (see *FL*, 395).

He carried the same rigidity of will into his religious service; the inner necessity which drove him in the first place to the Jesuit order carried him to extremes of abnegation and suffering within the order. Most of the time he allowed comfort no root-room at all; in times of reluctance, lethargy and depression he relied simply on will-power to force him through duties, resolutions and spiritual exercises. His private retreat notes are full of this bleak striving:

I must ask God to strengthen my faith or I shall never keep the particular examen. I must say the stations for this intention. Resolve also to keep it particularly even in the present state of lethargy.
(*S*, 256)

Consider your own misery and try as best you can to rise above it, by punctuality, and the particular examen; by fervour at office, mass and litanies; by good scholastic work; by charity if you get opportunities.
(*S*, 257)

It seemed to Hopkins that the Christian life was inevitably the way of heightened consciousness, therefore of greater pain. 'The keener the consciousness the greater the pain,' he wrote,

The greater the stress of being the greater the pain: both these show that the higher the nature the greater the penalty.
(*S*, 138)

Despite the inevitable 'penalty' he strove to 'pitch' or 'stress' his nature Godwards, to become perfect in obedience, and indifferent to pain, depression and frustration. Perfection in the service of God, according to St Ignatius, the founder of the Society of Jesus, means total self-abnegation;

... it is necessary to make ourselves indifferent in regard to all created things in so far as it is left to the choice of our free will and there is no prohibition; in such sort that we do not on our part seek for health rather than sickness, for riches rather than poverty, for honour rather than dishonour, for a long life rather than a short one; and so in all other things, desiring and choosing only those which may better lead us to the end for which we were created.

('The Principle or Foundation', *S*, 122)

Hopkins strove with fearful rigour to obey this regime to the letter. Even in the midst of desolations he prayed in 1883 to be lifted to a 'higher state of grace', to be freer from sin, and more zealous to do God's will, knowing that this would probably increase his pain and lift him 'on a higher cross' (*S*, 254)—as indeed it did. His nature took its revenge against this rigour by the torments of 1884-5, causing him to pray in March 1884: '*Facere nos indifferentes*—with the elective will, not the affective essentially; but the affective will will follow' (*S*, 256). The prayer reflects a mixture of desperation at the severity of his trials plus the stubborn hope that his nature will consent to be thus dominated.

This straining rigour which relies on naked will-power (the elective will) and rides rough-shod over desire, impulse and inclination (the affective will) is a distortion of true spirituality. It is perhaps a noble distortion, but it can be lacerating and destructive to the personality. It can turn life into a savage and weary grind, almost unbearable. In some notes belonging to these years Hopkins transcribed the following lines from Caradoc's soliloquy (from Act II of his unfinished drama *St Winefred's Well*):

> But will flesh, O can flesh
Second this fiery strain? Not always; O no no.
We cannot live this life out; sometimes we must weary
And in this darksome world what comfort can I find?
. . . .
I all my being have hacked in half with her neck.

(Quoted, *S*, 219)

There is no doubt that in Hopkins's case much of his exhaustion, depression and aridity was due to the unbending tyranny of his ideals, and his late decision to be to his 'sad self hereafter kind', had it come earlier, would have saved him a lot of distress.

Certainly one cannot blame the Society of Jesus for his state. The order is severe but is not inhuman. In the nineteenth century it was doubtless affected by the kind of Jansenism that stems from the Kantian categorical imperative and makes a complete opposition between duty and inclination. But Hopkins himself, judging by the schooldays reminiscences of Luxmoore, was a fanatic for duty from early days. In another age—say the twelfth century—he would have been trained in a deeper, more mystical spirituality in which the hardness of his will and the sensitivity of his nature would have been better blended. In the age of St Bernard or of Richard of St Victor his heart's energies might have flowered instead of grating on themselves.

As it is, however, we have these sonnets of torment and laceration, all of which are masterpieces, some of which 'came like inspirations unbidden' and against his will (*B*, 221). The sometimes laborious complexities of sprung rhythm, the strange alliterations, the odd word usages have been replaced by a compressed but much smoother diction, and a standard rhythm with rich variation of stress, much more 'Miltonic' as he wished his mature work to be. Each poem has been given a fairly full documentation, autobiographical as well as literary.

(*Carrion Comfort*)
(probably 1885)

Written probably in 1885, when Hopkins had barely emerged from a long period of depression and desolation. 'To judge of my case', he wrote to Bridges in May 1885, 'I think that my fits of sadness, though they do not affect my judgment, resemble madness. Change is the only relief, and that I can seldom get' (*B*, 216). The depression was so severe and so weakening, that he wrote to Bridges in 1884, after a bad attack: 'I did not know, but I was dying' (*B*, 193).

Bridges suggested that this is the sonnet of which Hopkins wrote: 'if ever anything was written in blood, one of these was'.

carrion comfort (line 1): because to abandon oneself to despair, though it brings a kind of relief, is to feed on spiritual death.

these last strands of man (line 2): see note to 'The Wreck of the Deutschland', st. 1, line 6, where Hopkins describes an early attack during which his innermost being 'gaped and fell apart . . . like a clod cleaving and holding only by strings of root'.

I can (line 3): i.e. do more. He is determined to oppose the crushing power of despair, by the sheer will to rise above it. In his life and belief Hopkins tended to hold too harsh an opposition between naked will power (the elective will) and the desires and inclinations of nature (the affective will). Father Devlin points out that much of his suffering was caused by this hidden perversity in this thinking (see *S*, 218).

Can something (line 4): i.e. can (do) something.

hope, wish day come, not choose not to be (line 4): the feeble but positive choices that the will can make in the face of despair. This mere choice to correspond to the will of God, 'this least sigh of desire, this one aspiration, is the life and spirit of man' ('On Personality, Grace and Free Will', *S*, 155).

O thou terrible (line 5): addressed to Christ rather than to the figure of Despair.

Wring-world, right foot rock (line 6): note swift violence of vowel run. See note on 'foot trod' (line 12) for ideas on the weight of Christ's tread. See also Job ix, 6.

lionlimb (line 6): see Job, x, 16 (*AV*).

bruisèd bones (line 7): cf. 'Barnfloor and Winepress' (1865) where Hopkins represents the body of Christ as

> *Bruised sore*
> *Scourged upon the threshing floor.*

This thought of scourging, threshing and of sacrifice, continued in Hopkins's own body and mind, underlies the rest of the poem.

fan (line 7): here used as a verb. In some retreat notes three years later Hopkins repeated and elucidated (perhaps unconsciously) the imagery of this poem. He wrote a meditation upon Luke, iii, 16–7 which contrasts the gentle baptism of John with the fearsome fire-and-Spirit baptism of Christ—'whose fan is in his hand and he will throughly purge his floor' (*AV*). The fan Hopkins defined as a large 'sort of scoop' in which the grain is tossed *violently* against the wind. The passage continues:

The separation it makes is very visible too: the grain *lies* heaped *on one side, the* chaff *blows away on the other, between them the winnower stands.*
(*S*, 267–8, Editor's roman)

It is obvious that Hopkins had long been trying to fit his torments into this context of baptism and purgation.

turns of tempest (line 8): see Job, ix, 17 (*AV*).

me frantic, etc. (line 8): Hopkins wrote in a spiritual diary 6 January 1885: 'For indeed it seems a spirit of fear I live by.' Thirteen days later came the pitiful entry: 'Pray not to be tormented' (*S*, 258–9).

Why? (line 9): In the sestet he answers the question posed in line 5. These fearsome attacks have a purifying effect; indeed, since he truly accepted them ('kissed the rod') they have brought joy.

kissed the rod (line 10): throughout his life, Hopkins strove, with his will, to make positive acceptance of his depressions as the will of God. A private meditation note of March 1884 reads:

Take it that weakness, ill health, every cross is a help. Calix quem Pater meus dedit mihi non bibam illum?[1]
(*S*, 256)

Hand rather (line 11): the hand (i.e. of God) wielding the rod of correction.

the hero (line 12): i.e. Christ—a frequent thought with Hopkins.

heaven-handling (line 12): providential ordering of the poet's existence.

foot trod (line 12): i.e. (whose) foot trod (me). In the retreat mentioned above which repeats so much of the imagery of this poem Hopkins meditated on the weight of Christ's foot *grinding* hard hearts to powder. He represents John the Baptist as saying: 'I tell you my fingers have not the force to *wring* open this man's laces' (*S*, 268. Editor's italics).

That night, that year (line 13): the night was like a year because of the intense torment. Speaking literally, 1884–5 was a whole year of darkness

[1] 'The cup which my father has given me, shall I not drink it'—John, 11. Christ's words just before his suffering.

for Hopkins. He writes in the poem that the darkness is 'now done', but wrote to Bridges in September 1885 that he feared its return:

Soon I am afraid I shall be ground down to a state like this last spring's and summer's, when my spirits were so crushed that madness seemed to be making approaches—and nobody was to blame, except myself partly for not managing myself better and contriving a change.

(*B*, 222)

(*my God!*) (line 14): A horrified whisper as he recalls the terror of that night.

Metre: A sonnet in sprung rhythm, 6 stresses per line. The following are outriding feet:

1.3, '*In me*'; 1.5, '*terrible*'; 1.8, '*tempest, me heaped there*'. L. 10 reads

'*Nay in all*'. 1.12, '*heaven-handling*'; 1.13, '*Me? or me*', and '*which one?*'.

Rhetorically, the poem is a masterpiece. Note the restless weaving of alliteration and internal rhyme, the constant shift of pace and mood, all capped and closed by the memorable last line.

'No worst, there is none'
(probably 1885)

Perhaps the most violent and hopeless of the sonnets of desolation. In most of the poems the suffering penetrates to archetypal depths, and contains echoes, conscious or otherwise, of Job, of Lear, and even of Milton's Satan. In this particular poem, however, the echoes are especially poignant, and nowhere, not even in 'Carrion Comfort', is Hopkins's despair at the crushing savagery of his spiritual torment better expressed.
Date: The autograph of the poem is on the same sheet as the third draft of 'Carrion Comfort', which would suggest 1885.

No worst, there is none (line 1): i.e. there is no such thing as 'worst'. Cf. Milton:

> . . . *infinite despair*
> *Which way I fly is Hell; myself am Hell;*
> *And, in the lowest deep, a lower deep*
> *Still threatening to devour me opens wide.*
> (*Paradise Lost*, Book IV, 75–8)

Pitched past pitch (line 1): 'pitched' and 'pitch' are rich words in this context. Apart from suggestions of blackness and of being hurled, the word in Hopkins's special usage meant also the 'stress' of highly wrought being, in this case his own mind. 'The keener the consciousness', he wrote, 'the greater the pain' ('Meditation on Hell', 1882, *S*, 138).

schooled at forepangs (line 2): lit. 'trained by previous pangs', the idea of torment increasing in violence and subtlety. In a private meditation on Hell, Hopkins wrote:

I remember in St Theresa's vision of Hell, to this effect: 'I know not how it is, but in spite of the darkness the eye sees there all that to see is most afflicting'. Against these acts of its own the lost spirit dashes itself like a caged bear and is in prison, violently instresses them and burns, stares into them and is deeper darkened.
('Long Retreat and later', 1881, *S*, 138)

Hopkins, of course, being a theologian, did not literally believe himself to be damned—see sonnet 'I wake and feel the fell of dark, not day', note on last line (p. 160)—but he knew his torments to be akin to those of the Hell in which he devoutly believed.

Comforter (line 3): a cry to the Holy Spirit.

Mary, mother of us (line 4): probably echoes of the Litany of the Blessed

Virgin where Mary is prayed to as Comforter of the afflicted and Help of Christians.

heave, herds-long (line 5): an odd image, but effective in conveying endless unrest. For Hopkins's physical as well as mental unrest see sonnet 'I wake and feel the fell of dark, not day', note on 'I am gall' etc. (line 9) (p. 159).

on an age-old anvil wince (line 6): the anvil is 'age-old' because the chosen man of God has always suffered, almost beyond endurance. Cf. Job., vi:

For the arrows of the Almighty are within me,
the poison whereof drinketh up my spirit:
the terrors of God do set themselves in array against me.
(verse 4).

. . . Oh that I might have my request; and that God would grant me the
thing that I long for.
Even that it would please God to destroy me.
(verses 8–9).

and sing (line 6): because, even while wincing with pain, the faithful soul has always tried to 'kiss the rod'—see 'Carrion Comfort'—and glorify God.

fell (line 8): swift and malevolent; there is a touch of Victorian melodrama here but the context holds it well.

force (line 8): i.e. perforce.

cliffs of fall/Frightful (lines 9–10): see Milton lines quoted above. There are many points at which Hopkins in his own experience anticipated the theories and discoveries of William James the psychologist, despite the difference of their basic philosophies. James illustrated with case histories the fact that the human mind, under certain conditions of stress and nervous derangement can lurch into an abyss of horror.

Not the conception or intellectual perception of evil, but the grisly blood-
freezing heart-palsying sensation of it close upon one, and no other conception
or sensation able to live for a moment in its presence. How irrelevantly
remote seem all our usual refined optimisms and intellectual and moral
consolations in presence of a need of help like this. Here is the real core of the
religious problem: Help! help!

(*Varieties of Religious Experience.* Longmans [London, 1911], p. 162)

There is no doubt that the tense and highly wrought mind of Hopkins was subject to such attacks, which plunged him beyond all rational comfort and religious support.

Nor does long our small/Durance, etc. (lines 11–12): cf. T. S. Eliot: 'Human kind cannot bear too much reality.'

Here! creep,/Wretch, etc. (lines 12–13): language reminiscent of the tormented Lear, houseless in the storm, creeping into a hovel.

all/Life does end, etc. (lines 13–14): this is his comfort in the whirlwind. Cf. Lear: 'Nay get thee in. I'll pray and then I'll sleep'. For full discussion of Shakespearian and other 'undertones' in these sonnets see *WHG*, Vol. I, pp. 175 et seq.

Metre: standard sonnet rhythm, but with such irregular stressing that the result is almost sprung rhythm—see metre notes on 'To seem the stranger'. Frequent heavy stressing of the first syllable of the line, inverting the iambic foot (∪–) to a trochaic (–∪), e.g. line 4: *Mary, mother of us;* line 10: *'Frightful, sheer';* also lines 12 and 13.

'To seem the stranger lies my lot, my life'
(1885)

This is one of the four sonnets found in Hopkins's papers after his death, referred to in the 1885 letter quoted in the notes to 'My own heart let me more have pity on' (p. 163).

Hopkins went to Ireland in February 1884 as Professor of Greek at the University College, Dublin. The feeling of being a stranger, however, went far deeper in Hopkins's case than an Englishman's exile in Ireland. As evidenced in that early and moving poem 'The Alchemist in the City', Hopkins had always been 'the stranger', curiously remote from himself and from his environment, and frequently at frustrating odds with both.

It was perhaps part of his suffering destiny that the last years of his life should be a very Gethsemane: a patriotic convert Englishman immersed unwillingly in Irish Jesuit enthusiasm for home rule; a scholar and poet so crushed by vast quantities of examination papers to mark that his vital energies were swamped; and a man of ability who had been the 'star of Balliol', increasingly subject to bouts of depression and weakness which sapped all hope of accomplishing anything.

This poem is a mild expression of that mood which was to intensify over the years and which culminated in the self-laceration of the 'straining eunuch' notes of 1888—see notes to 'Thou art indeed just, Lord' (p. 178). In the end it was not the fact of being a stranger that hurt him, but rather the total frustration and failure (as he thought) of all he ever hoped to do.

are in Christ not near (line 3): Hopkins's family were devout Anglicans, and his parents had bitterly opposed his conversion to Rome in 1866. 'Their answers are terrible: I cannot read them twice,' he wrote to Newman at the time (*FL*, 29).

And he my peace my parting, sword and strife (line 4): i.e. 'and he (Christ) who is peace to me is also sword and strife'. Cf. Christ's words recorded by Matthew: 'I came not to send peace but a sword' (Matt., x, 34). Cf. also Hopkins's own anguished questioning of this mystery of Christ's dealings with his followers in 'Carrion Comfort' and in 'Thou art indeed just, Lord'.

England, whose honour O all my heart woos (line 5): Hopkins was an ardent patriot. In 1885, the year of this poem, he also wrote the song 'What shall I do for the land that bred me?' It is a jingoistic jingle, but he meant it with all his heart. The final stanza runs:

Call me England's fame's fond lover,
Her fame to keep, her fame to recover.
Spend me, or end me what God shall send me
But under her banner I live for her honour.

wife/To my creating thought (lines 5–6): the idea that England was the sole fruitful source of his poetic inspiration and that outside England he was barren, was, as Father Devlin remarks, a little self-delusion produced by his over-driven nature. Hopkins realized this himself, later. He wrote to Bridges in 1887:

. . . But out of Ireland I shd. be no better, rather worse probably. I only need one thing—a working health, a working strength: with that any employment is tolerable or pleasant, enough for human nature; without it, things are liable to go very hardly with it.

(B. 251)

would neither hear/Me, were I pleading (lines 6–7): i.e. about 'what a mess Ireland is and how everything enters into that mess', as he later put it to his mother (*FL*, 184). Hopkins, though patriotic, was not unsympathetic to the Irish cause; he stood by helplessly and saw blindness and bigotry on both sides.

third/Remove (lines 9–10): Hopkins had had many more than three moves in the course of his training and work. Possibly here he means a threefold removal from his roots, i.e. from his family, from the Anglican faith and from England.

Only what word, etc. (lines 11–13): the sense is roughly 'If only it were not for the fact that the best that I have in me finds no utterance, being thwarted either by a mysterious providence or by evil powers'. He wrote later to Bridges:

I am in a position which makes it befitting and almost a duty to write anything (bearing on classical study) which I may feel that I could treat well and advance learning by: there is such a subject; I do try to write at it; but I see that I cannot get on, that I shall be even less able hereafter than now. And of course if I cannot do what even my appliances make best and easiest, far less can I do anything else. Still I could throw myself cheerfully into my day's work? I cannot, I am in a prostration.

(B, 251)

leaves me a lonely began (line 14): a most desolate-sounding line, leaving a half-picture in the mind of a solitary figure left at a starting post, all others having finished their race. Dr Gardner suggests, for 'began', a comparison with the noun 'also-ran' (notes to Penguin edition).

Metre: standard sonnet rhythm, i.e. 5 iambic feet per line, but lines 5–8 are so freely counterpointed and the stresses so unevenly distributed that they could be called 'sprung'. This sonnet, like the rest of the group is notable for the compression and sinewed flexibility of the diction which, combined with the alliterations and the lettering of the vowels, shows Hopkins's distinctive genius in the handling of the English language.

'I wake and feel the fell of dark, not day'
(probably 1885)

The sufferings of Hopkins were deep and intense, and his thoughts, even his words, often echo those of the archetypal figures of agony, Lear and Job. Had this poem had an epigraph it might well have come from Job's description of his nightly torments:
When I say, My bed shall comfort me,
   my couch shall ease my complaint;
Then thou scarest me with dreams;
   and terrifiest me through visions:
So that my soul chooseth strangling,
   and death rather than life.
I loathe it; I would not live alway:
Let me alone; for my days are vanity.
(vii, 13–16)
fell (line 1): a multi-valued word. 'Fell', as adj. = malevolent; as noun = hairy skin as of a beast. There is probably an echo of Macbeth, as W. H. Gardner suggests:
      . . . my sense would have cooled
To hear a night-shriek; and my fell of hair
Would at a dismal treatise rouse and stir
As life were in't.
(*Macbeth*, V, v, 10–12)
black hours (line 2): such as described in 'Carrion Comfort' and 'No worse, there is none', when Hopkins was tormented by self-loathing, tempted by suicidal impulses, and crushed by despair approaching madness.
I mean years, mean life (line 6): years in the sense that Hopkins's bouts of depression increased in length and intensity as he became older, and also in the sense that each attack, in itself, seemed an eternity of misery with time stretched out intolerably before and after.
   'Soon', he wrote to Bridges, 'I am afraid I shall be ground down to a state like this last spring's and summer's, when my spirits were so crushed that madness seemed to be making approaches' (*B*, 222).
And more must, etc. (line 4): i.e. his heart must spend more 'black hours' if daylight delays.
like dead letters (line 7): the feeling of being totally cut off from God and from all comfort has been suffered by many in the religious state. St Ignatius called it 'spiritual desolation' and described it as follows:

... darkness and confusion of soul, attraction towards low and earthly objects, disquietude caused by various agitations and temptations, which move the soul to diffidence without hope and without love, so that it finds itself altogether slothful, tepid, sad, and as it were separated from its Creator and Lord.

(Rules for the Discernment of Spirits, IV; *S*, 204)

I am gall, I am heartburn (line 9): this imagery of acute physical malaise and discomfort is not merely symbolic of Hopkins's inner state of mind. His whole being—body and mind—was sick and enervated at these times. 'The body cannot rest when it is in pain', he wrote on retreat in 1888, 'nor the mind be at peace as long as something bitter distils in it and it aches' (*S*, 262).

my taste was me (line 10): in some philosophical notes of 1880, Hopkins had written of the incommunicable 'feel' of self-conscousness:

... above all my shame, my guilt, my fate are the very things in feeling, in tasting, which I most taste that selftaste which nothing in the world can match.

(Meditation on First Principle or Foundation; *S*, 125. Editor's roman)

Frequently throughout his life this 'selftaste' to Hopkins brought unbearable self-loathing. He wrote on retreat in 1888:

I was continuing this train of thought this evening when I began to enter on that course of loathing and hopelessness which I have so often felt before, which made me fear madness and led me to give up the practice of meditation except, as now, in retreat and here it is again.

(*S*, 262)

Selfyeast of spirit a dull dough sours (line 12): a vivid image of a spiritual sickness when the sense of oppression is so great that something physically clammy, lumpish and sour seems to have settled on the spirit. William James (see sonnet 'No worst, there is none', p. 153; note on 'cliffs of fall', lines 9–10) analysed and documented this state, which he called anhedonia. It is a loss of all life and joy, a suffocating feeling of futility, an almost tangible awareness of being damned and a sense that Heaven is 'a vacuum; a mythological elysium, an abode of shadows less real than the earth'. Those who strive for perfection in the religious state are especially prone to it. In Hopkins's case the frequent—and sometimes mistaken—forcing of his nature by his will contributed to his condition. He totally exhausted his nervous resources.

their sweating selves (line 14): in sermon notes on Hell, Hopkins dwelt on the total self-isolation of the damned, left alone with their own tormenting souls:

It is still the same story: they, *their sins are the bitterness, tasted sweet once,*

now taste most bitter; no worm but themselves gnaws them and gnaws no one but themselves.
(*S*, 243)
The idea is traditional, but Hopkins, from experience, drew it to a fine point.

but worse (line 14): Hopkins, being theologically accurate, never believed himself to be in hell, but he believed his experiences to be akin to the torments that the damned suffer. The latter are only 'worse' because they include feelings of remorse and endless loss:

... taste as with taste of tongue all that is bitter there, the tears ceaselessly and fruitlessly flowing; the grief over their hopeless loss; the worm of conscience, which is the mind gnawing and feeding on its own miserable self.
(*S*, 243)
He clung meanwhile to his hope of Heaven. It gave him a kind of certainty but none of the comfort he badly needed. In his retreat notes of 1888, he wrote:

There is a happiness, hope, the anticipation of happiness hereafter; it is better than happiness, but it is not happiness now. It is as if one were dazzled by a spark or star in the dark, seeing it but not seeing by it: we want a light shed on our way and a happiness spread over our life.
(*S*, 262)

Metre: standard metre with fairly free distribution of the stresses. Elisions at line 8 'I͡ am gall, I͡ am heartburn'.

'Patience, hard thing! the hard thing but to pray'
(1885)

'*Let him who is in desolation*', *wrote St Ignatius, founder of the Society of Jesus, 'strive to remain in patience, which is the virtue contrary to the troubles which harass him; and let him think that he will shortly be consoled, making diligent efforts against the desolation, as has been said in the sixth rule.*'
(Rules for the Discernment of Spirits, VIII; *S*, 204)

See notes to 'Thou art indeed just, Lord, if I contend' (p. 178) for the circumstances of Hopkins's frustration—a stranger in Ireland, unwillingly associated with the (to him) unlawful and uninteresting cause of Home Rule, and lacking even the basic essentials of 'bodily energy and cheerful spirits'.

but to pray (line 1): i.e. even to pray for patience is hard, because, as he explains in the next lines, he who is forced to ask for patience really would prefer the relief of outward strife and action. In an order which was organized 'to fight and not to heed the wounds', it was given to Hopkins to fight only interior battles, an infinitely harder 'war'.

weary his times, his tasks (line 3): the religious life, to Hopkins, was frequently an obscure grind, freely chosen but barely tolerable in his frequent bouts of nervous prostration. Above all, after his appointment as Professor of Greek in Dublin, the enormous number of examination papers he had to mark yearly weighed upon his mind. 'It is killing work to examine a nation,' he wrote. His letters during these years are punctuated by gasps and groans, often amusingly phrased, but obviously the cries of one consistently taxed beyond his strength.

To do without, take tosses, and obey (line 4): Hopkins might have been a noted preacher, but just failed, somehow, to bring it off; or a classical scholar, but he lacked the time and energy to bring any original work to full fruition; or a recognized poet, but he refused, perhaps perversely, all chances of recognition. Even his ambition to do great things for his master, Christ, were thwarted by circumstances, by ill health and perhaps by his own temperament. He meditated and prayed on the injunction '*Facere nos indifferentes*'[1] on his last retreat, but right to the end he found it bitterly hard. The poignant words of a very early poem proved to be prophetic:

Yet it is now too late to heal
The incapable and cumbrous shame

[1] '*Facere nos indifferentes*'—the first Rule and Principle of St. Ignatius is 'to make ourselves indifferent in regard to all created things'.

Which makes me when with men I deal
More powerless than the blind or lame.
('The Alchemist in the City')
these (line 5): i.e. in doing without, taking tosses, etc.

Natural heart's ivy (line 6): a satisfying image of a slow, soft, concealing growth spreading over cracks and bareness.

Purple eyes, etc. (line 8): soft and sensuous both in image and sound, suggesting a Hopkins trying to treat himself more kindly.

We hear our hearts grate (line 9): a harsh contrast to the soft lull of the previous line. During a ruthless self-examination on retreat early in 1889, he wrote of the work he had been doing in Dublin for the last five years: 'I am not willing enough for the piece of work assigned me.'

Yet the rebellious wills, etc. (lines 10–11): as Father Devlin points out it was not his will but his outraged nature, over-driven by his will, that was in rebellion. See 'Carrion Comfort' (p. 149) (note on 'I can', line 3) for Hopkin's tendency to crush and thwart his nature with his 'elective' will, a tendency derived neither from Scotus nor from Ignatius, but rather from bleak Victorian ethics which drew a far too severe distinction between duty and inclination.

Delicious kindness (line 13): this thought, plus the imagery of bees and honey following, recalls the psalmist who prays for the 'kindness' of God (Ps. cxix, 73) and to whom the words of the Lord are 'sweeter than honey' (verse 103). 'Comb' = honeycomb.

those ways we know (line 14): St Ignatius laid down that the victim of desolation should stand firm, and that he should adopt some means of bearing with this state—more prayer and meditation, more accurate self-examination, a realization that God may be testing the quality of the victim's love by withdrawing all consolation, and the realization that He sends consolation and withdraws it according to His will, not the will of His follower. All this may be somewhat cold comfort but it steels the will to patience.

. . . great gifts and great opportunities are more than life spares to one man.
. . . [wrote Hopkins to Dixon]. *Above all Christ our Lord: his career was cut short, and whereas he would have wished to succeed by success—for it is insane to lay yourself out for failure . . . nevertheless he was doomed to succeed by failure; his plans were baffled, his hopes dashed, and his work was done by being broken off undone. However much he understood all this he found it an intolerable grief to submit to it. He left the example: it is very strengthening, but except in that sense it is not consoling.*
(*D*, 137–8)

Metre: standard metre, but heavily and irregularly stressed in the manner of 'To seem the stranger' (q.v.).

This is very probably one of the sonnets referred to in a letter to Bridges of 1 September 1885:

I shall shortly have some sonnets to send you, five or more. Four of these came like inspirations unbidden and against my will. And in the life I lead now, which is one of a continually jaded and harassed mind, if in any leisure I try to do anything I make no way—nor with my work, alas, but so it must be.
(*B*, 221)

It was found among Hopkins's posthumous papers, written on a small sheet which also contained 'To seem the stranger lies my lot, my life', 'I wake and feel the fell of dark, not day', 'Patience, hard thing'! the hard thing but to pray', and a poem which Bridges entitled 'Ash-boughs'. Certainly from the mood of the poem—a mind gasping in its own torment and groping for comfort—the year 1885 would be a likely date.

Father Devlin suggests that it was written towards the end of a long and particularly savage period of stress when his spirits had been crushed to a state approaching madness—see notes on 'Carrion Comfort' (p. 149). A simple entry in a private retreat note of January 1885 bespeaks his tortured mind at the time: 'The devils who tormented the demoniac—pray not to be tormented' (*S*, 259). Father Devlin points out that although some of Hopkins's sufferings were definitely caused by a half-hidden perversity and wilfulness in his own nature, it is not hard to believe that they were part of the mystery of his sanctification (see *S*, 219–20).

The poem is an attempt at self-consolation. He instructs himself to be a little more kind to his own human nature and to cease the endless morbid introspection that is eating away his life. He urges himself to cease anticipating endless misery in order to leave room for the small unexpected joys that come unbidden.

to my sad self (line 2): a letter to Bridges of April 1885 speaks of 'that coffin of weakness and dejection in which I live' (*B*, 214–15).
With this tormented mind tormenting yet (line 4): for a description of the fits of self-loathing that drove Hopkins to thoughts of madness or suicide, see opening notes to 'Thou art indeed just, Lord, if I contend' (p. 178). For descriptions of the violence of his torments, see notes on 'No worst, there is none' (pp. 152–3) and 'I wake and feel the fell of dark, not day' (p. 158).
than blind/Eyes in their dark, etc. (lines 6–8): extending Bridge's partial elucidation of this passage, the sense is 'I grope for comfort I can no

more get than blind eyes in their dark can get daylight, or thirst can find relief in the midst of the ocean'. The latter analogy sounds like an echo of Coleridge's ancient mariner who found 'water, water everywhere, but not a drop to drink'.

poor Jackself (line 9): he addresses his own drudging, over-conscientious, workaday self, the Hopkins who, in Ireland had' done God's will (in the main) and many examination papers' (quoted by Dr Gardner, *WHG*, Vol. I, 119).

call off thoughts awhile (line 10): Hopkins had spoken in 'Spelt from Sibyl's Leaves' and elsewhere of the endless grinding of thought upon thought that was part of his affliction and, greatly intensified, part of the tortures of the damned.

let joy size, etc. (lines 11–12): the sense is 'let joy spring up and grow whenever and however God wills it'.

whose smile|'s not wrung (lines 12–13): i.e. whose favours cannot be forced from him.

Betweenpie (line 14): i.e. 'to dapple in between'. Bridges noted this usage as:
... a strange word, in which pie *apparently makes a compound verb with* between, *meaning 'as the sky seen between dark mountains is brightly dappled', the grammar such as* intervariegates *would make.*
(Notes to 1st edition, p. 117)
He added, somewhat impatiently:
This word might have delighted William Barnes, if the verb 'to pie' existed. It seems not to exist, and to be forbidden by homophonic absurdities.
(ibid.)
Dr Gardner, however, defends it as follows:
But for G.M.H. the verb 'to pie' did exist—as a 'back-formation, from magpie or 'pied': in notebooks, p. 176, he speaks of 'white pieings' on the 'dull thunder-colour' of pigeons.
(Notes to 3rd edition)
Finally, putting linguistics aside, the sort of thing Hopkins probably meant, may be found in his early Journal:
In the gap between the hills was Dartmoor and the country between in the foreground of it/all in blue, the woods in mosaic of deeper blue. I have forgotten even now much but this was a very beautiful sight.
(*J*, 252)

Metre: a sonnet which seems to be in standard rhythm in the octet, but which expands into sprung rhythm in the sestet. For remarks on the highly wrought quality of the diction see metre notes on 'To seem the stranger lies my lot, my life' (p. 157).

Tom's Garland
(Dromore, September 1887)

This is a companion poem to 'Harry Ploughman', and equally difficult. Certainly neither Bridges nor Canon Dixon understood it, and Bridges had to write for a 'crib'. 'I laughed outright and often, but very sardonically', replied Hopkins,

. . . to think you and the Canon could not construe my last sonnet; that he had to write to you for a crib. It is plain I must go no farther on this road; if you and he cannot understand me who will?

(*B*, 272)

He insisted, as always, that the poem was to be read aloud, and even 'declaimed', in which case 'the strange constructions would be dramatic and effective'. He finished his lengthy explanation, with the slightly rueful verdict:

I think it is a very pregnant sonnet and in point of execution very highly wrought. Too much so, I am afraid.

(*B* 274)

The theme of the poem is the happiness of those who accept their place, however humble, in a commonwealth, and the rage and misery of those who can find no place in it. The notion of commonweal had been developed by Hopkins in sermons and meditations, and he explained it as follows to Bridges:

. . . as St Paul and Plato and Hobbes and everyone says, the commonwealth or well-ordered society is like one man; a body with many members and each its function; some higher, some lower, but all honourable, from the honour that belongs to the whole. The head is the sovereign, who has no superior but God and from heaven receives his or her authority . . . The foot is the daylabourer, and this is armed with hobnail boots, because it has to wear and be worn by the ground; which again is symbolical: for it is navvies or daylabourers who, on the great scale or in gangs and millions, mainly trench, tunnel, blast, and in other ways disfigure, 'mammock' the earth and . . . stamp it with their footprints.

(*B*, 272–3)

The 'Tom' of the poem is a navvy, and the 'garland' he wears turns out to be the nails in his boots. Of Tom and his ilk, Hopkins continued:

And the 'garlands' of nails they wear are therefore the visible badge of the place they fill, the lowest in the commonwealth. But this place still shares the common honour, and if it wants one advantage, glory or public fame, makes up for it by another, ease of mind, absence of care; and these things

are symbolized by the gold and the iron garlands. (O, once explained, how clear it all is!)
(ibid.)

garlanded (line 1): explained above but, like some of the images in 'Harry Ploughman', it tends to give a misleading visual impression, at first reading.

fallowbootfellow (line 2): Dick is Tom's 'bootfellow', his friend and fellow navvy. He is 'fallow', i.e. idle, because it is the end of the day. Hopkins continued his explanation:

. . . the scene of the poem is laid at evening, when they are giving over work and one after another pile their picks, with which they earn their living, and swing off home, knocking sparks out of mother earth . . . taking all easy. And so to supper and bed.
(ibid.)

This will explain 'piles pick' (line 2) and 'rips out rockfire homeforth' (line 3).

lustily he his low lot . . . swings though (lines 5–8): omitting the poet's half-envious comment contained in the brackets, 'swings his low lot' means 'surveys his lot, but free from care; then by a sudden strong act throws it over the shoulder or tosses it away as a light matter' (ibid.).

(feel/That ne'er need hunger, Tom, etc.) (lines 5–8): a typical inversion of word order, producing a rhythmical phrase where awkwardness might otherwise have resulted. In these lines in brackets, the poet, himself frequently ailing and troubled by 'thousands of thorns, thoughts', marvels at Tom's immunity from these burdens.

Commonweal/Little I reck ho (lines 8–9): this passage down to 'mighty foot' is what Hopkins described as 'a violent but effective hyperbaton or suspension, in which the action of the mind mimics that of the labourer' (ibid.). These words are supposed to be Tom's thoughts as he thinks them. The sense is: 'I don't waste any time thinking about the commonweal, as I would be low in status ("lacklevel") in even the best society. Belonging to a well ordered country is honour enough for me, whether at the head or the foot' (see above, introduction to the poem).

But no way sped (line 12): from here, to the end of the poem, Hopkins turns to the lot of those who, either from their own or society's fault, have no place in the commonwealth. Like a patriotic Tory, he has so far, in the mouth of Tom, defended the status quo. Now he remembers the other side:

But presently I remember that this is all very well for those who are in, however low in, the Commonwealth and share in any way the common weal;

but that the curse of our times is that many do not share it, that they are
outcasts from it and have neither security nor splendour; that they share
care with the high and obscurity with the low, but wealth or comfort with
neither. And this state of things, I say, is the origin of Loafers, Tramps,
Cornerboys, Roughs, Socialists and other pests of society.
(ibid., 273–4)
From this explanation we may construct the following very loose paraphrase set below the relevant portion of the text:

<pre>
                     But no way sped,
                     But there are those who are not employed
Nor mind nor mainstrength; gold go garlanded
Either in mind or body;   who neither carry the dangerous burden
With perilous, O no; nor yet plod safe shod sound.
Of wealth (power);   nor toil safely at lower levels of society;
                     Undenizened beyond bound
                     Disinherited, cast out from the glories
Of earth's glory, earth's ease, all;   no one, nowhere.
and even from the comforts of life, from everything; with no identity, no place
In wide the world's weal;   rare gold, bold steel, bare
In the general welfare of society; having neither wealth nor a working man's
                     In both; care, but share care—
                     Job;   sharing only the worries that all have
</pre>

This, by Despair, bred Hangdog dull (line 19): 'This' refers to the 'care'
or anxiety of their state which has caused despair and turned them into
the tramps and loafers mentioned above. Or their state has caused rage
and turned them into rebels and 'Socialists', by which Hopkins meant
anarchists and wreckers. He is not to be taken as High Tory or anti-
Socialist (in the present-day sense of the word). In fact in a famous letter
of 1871 to Bridges, he wrote:
Horrible to say, in a manner I am a Communist. Their ideal bating some
things is nobler than that professed by any secular statesman I know of (I
must own I live in a bat-light and shoot at a venture). Besides it is just.—
I do not mean the means of getting to it are. But it is a dreadful thing for
the greatest and most necessary part of a very rich nation to live a hard
life without dignity, knowledge, comforts, delight, or hopes in the midst of
plenty—which plenty they make. They profess that they do not care what
they wreck and burn, the old civilization and order must be destroyed. This
is a dreadful look out but what has the old civilization done for them?
(*B*, 27–8)

Metre: common sonnet rhythm (iambic pentameter) but with 'hurried
feet'—see metrical notes to 'Harry Ploughman' for explanation of this
term. The hurried feet marked in the manuscripts are:

1.3 *By him and rips*

1.5 *Low be it: lustily he his low lot*

1.10 *Country is honour enough in all us.*

This is a 'caudated' or 'caudal' sonnet, i.e. it has two codas or additions following the basic fourteen lines. The codas are the three lines beginning 'Undenizened' and the further three beginning 'In both'. Hopkins's model was Milton's sonnet 'On the New Forcers of Conscience'.

Harry Ploughman
(Dromore, September 1887)

Writing to Dixon in December 1887, enclosing this poem and 'Tom's Garland', Hopkins said:

I enclose two sonnets, works of infinite, of over great contrivance, I am afraid, to the annulling in the end of the right effect. They have also too much resemblance to each other; but they were conceived at the same time. They are of a 'robustious' sort . . . They are meant for, and cannot properly be taken in without, emphatic recitation; which nevertheless is not an easy performance.

(D, 153)

'I want Harry Ploughman to be a vivid picture before the mind's eye', he wrote to Bridges, 'if he is not that the sonnet fails. The difficulties are of syntax no doubt' *(B, 265)*. Indeed the syntax is twisted and involuted to the point of discomfort, and Hopkins admitted that he could go no farther along this particular road.

Furthermore, the poem can hardly be called a 'picture' in the sense of a pictorial impression conveyed through simple, vivid pictorial imagery. It is the compressed tortuousness of the syntax, and the forceful but controlled irregularities of rhythm that help to evoke the physique and movements of a powerfully muscled man. There is something in this poem comparable to a Michelangelo drawing of the male physique, with the muscle patterns accentuated. The total impression is gained, however, through sound, rhythm and association, rather than through simple pictorial imagery.

broth of goldish flue/Breathed round (lines 1–2): 'flue' = downy hair. The sense is of light golden, downy, breezeblown hairs on Harry's arms.
scooped flank (line 2): i.e. slim waist; 'scooped' because forming a graceful concave curve between ribs and hip.
lank/Rope-over thigh (lines 2–3): lean and heavily muscled thigh.
knee-nave (line 3): knee-cap. Originally 'knee-bank' but changed probably for alliterative effect. It can mean 'centre'—otherwise it contributes very little, either pictorially or logically.
barrelled shank (line 3): calves bulging with muscle. Hopkins has dwelt on the varying muscularity of Harry's body, 'scooped', 'lank', and 'barrelled'.
Head and foot, shoulder and shank (line 4): this, and the other four short lines in the poem, Hopkins described as 'burden lines', saying that they might be recited as chorus *(B, 263)*. The elements of chorus and solemn

refrain in this poem make it more a Pindaric ode than a descriptive sonnet, despite Hopkins's assertion that it is meant to be 'a direct picture of a ploughman without afterthought' (*B*, 262).

By a grey eye's heed steered well, one crew, etc. (line 5): all the limbs of Harry's body are envisaged as 'one crew' at the fall-in position, ready for orders. Each has its allotted 'sinew-service' or function in the whole body, a curious carry-over, from 'Tom's Garland', of the idea of Commonwealth.

barrowy (line 6): suggests thickness and solidity.

onewhere curded, onewhere sucked or sank (line 7): refers to the different muscles of lines 1–4. 'Curded' = knotted.

beechbole (line 9): the trunk of a beech.

And features, in flesh, what deed (line 10): the appearance of each muscle is a guide to what function it performs.

He leans to it, etc. (line 12): there is excitement and acceleration as Harry swings into action. The language becomes dynamic: 'quail', 'hurls', 'lashed', 'raced', 'shining-shot'.

quail (line 13): a very expressive word evoking the bracing and giving-way movements of a ploughman as he keeps himself and his heavy implement in equilibrium.

crossbridle (line 14): lift and tangle. Refers to his 'curls'.

wind- lilylocks -laced (line 15): i.e. his windblown white hair. Putting 'lilylocks' in the middle of 'wind-laced' is a device called tmesis, the intention being to 'inscape' in a single piece of language the single impression of Harry's hair in the wind.

Churlsgrace (line 16): 'Churl' = peasant (Old English).

Amansstrength (line 16): simply 'a man's strength' but, thus inscaped, and with capital letter, evokes something stark and elemental about his appearance, like elemental Man or a primitive Norse god.

how it hangs or hurls/Them, etc. (lines 16–19): a passage of incomparable tortuousness. 'It' refers to 'churlsgrace', Harry's peasant strength. 'Them' refers to the 'furls' or furrows curling, sometimes slowly, sometimes at furious speed, from the plough. The sense is as follows: '(See how) his peasant grace, born of strength, hangs or hurls them over—cold furrows, the ploughshare ("cragiron") beneath them, his feet keeping pace beside and along them—furrows which are "shot" (flecked) with "shining" (gleaming) like a fountain.' Hopkins remarked:

Dividing a compound word by a clause sandwiched into it was a desperate deed, I feel, and I do not feel that it was an unquestionable success.
(*B*, 265)

broad in bluff hide his frowning feet lashed (line 17): an additional adjectival group of words round 'feet' which adds further to the complexity of the

passage above. W. H. Gardner (Penguin edition, p. 244) suggests that
'frowning' refers to the 'frowning wrinkles' in Harry's boots. The suggestion is also, probably, of a heavy-booted tread upon the earth, another
carry-over from 'Tom's Garland'. 'Broad' is adjectival to the 'bluff hide'
(strong leather) of the boots that 'lash' or encase his feet.

Metre: Hopkins issued an elaborate metrical notation to this poem
(facsimile, *B*, 262) and wrote to Bridges on the desirability of a kind of
syntactical notation: 'to distinguish the subject, verb, object and in general
to express the construction to the eye; as is done already partly in punctua-
tion by everybody, partly in capitals by the Germans, more fully in
accentuation by the Hebrews' (*B*, 265).

The metre is sprung rhythm with 5 basic stresses per line. The rhythm
is 'heavily loaded' however, with,

1. *Hurried feet*, consisting of 2, 3, or 4 syllables, crammed into the time

of one: e.g. *Though as a beechbole firm*, l. 9; *his, as at a roll-call, rank*, l. 9.
2. *Outriding feet*, i.e. stresses additional to the number expected which
break the rhythm by their emphasis, but which at the same time must be
discounted in the mind. Hopkins marked them with the usual nether
loop.⌣ e.g. *In him, all quail*, l. 13;

Churlsgrace, too, child of Amansstrength, **l. 16.**

After the outriders, the voice pauses slightly as if it were 'silently making
its way back to the highroad of the verse' (*B*, opp. 262).
Hopkins's notation, plus his comments, is as follows:

- Λ : strong stress; which does not differ much from
- ⋒ : pause or dwell on a syllable, which need not however have the metrical stress.
- ⁄ : the metrical stress, marked in doubtful cases only.
- ⌣ : quiver or circumflexion, making one syllable nearly two, most used with diphthongs and vowels.
- ⌢ : between syllables stress them into one.
- ⌒ : over three or more syllables gives them the time of one half foot.
- ⌣ : the outride (see above).

For a full discussion of Hopkins's 'code' for this and other poems see
WHG, Vol. I, p. 90, et seq.

That Nature is a Heraclitean Fire and of the
Comfort of the Resurrection
(26 July 1888)

Written at Dublin, July 1888. Only one MS. and that rather provisional.

Heraclitean Fire: The ancient Greek philosopher Heraclitus, who lived
c. 500 B.C., taught that an ethereal fire was the ultimate constituent of the
universe:

This world, which is the same for all, no one of gods or men has made:
but it was ever, is now and ever shall be an ever-living Fire, with measures
kindling and measures going out.

He also taught that the energy and beauty of this world is generated
through an endless clash and tension of opposites:

God is day and night, winter and summer, war and peace, surfeit and hunger.
Hopkins had read much early Greek philosophy and was attracted by
this kind of teaching, being himself sensitive to the enormous energies
in nature and aware of the creative/destructive tensions in his own
make up.

   Argument: Nature is an endless and ever-changing movement of light
and shadow, air, water and earth. Man himself seems part of this process.
No matter how unique a creation he is, he is destined for oblivion like
everything else. This sombre train of thought is interrupted by the joyful
and saving thought of Christ's Resurrection. Man will not die because
through Christ he is assured of immortality.

Cloud-puffball, torn tufts, etc. (lines 1–4): cloudscapes were an endless
source of fascination to Hopkins judging by frequent entries in his Journal
where words like 'tufts', 'pillow', 'tossed', 'snowy', 'meal-white', 'bright',
'flashing' are used in description.

chevy (line 1): chase.

heaven-roysterers (line 2): In a Journal entry of 1871 Hopkins described
clouds as 'slanted flashing "travellers", all in flight, stepping one behind
the other, their edges tossed with bright ravelling' (*J*, 207).

in marches (line 2): another recurring thought to Hopkins. Cf. his description of clouds 'marching across the sky in regular rank' near Pendle Hill.

Down roughcast, etc. (line 3): I think this refers simply to the movement of
cloud shadow on walls and buildings.

Shivelights (line 4): slivers, splinters or shafts of light.

shadowtackle (line 4): sunlight through tree branches throwing a shadow
patterned like the rigging of a ship. Cf. *J*, 192:

The hangers of smaller but barky branches, seen black against the leaves from within, look like ship-tackle.

lace, lance, and pair (line 4): all verbs, evoking the endless movement of shafted light through tree foliage, on a windswept, bright, cloud-driven day.

bright wind (line 5): exactly the effect of energy of air and light he is trying to create. 'Wind' is the subject of the following verbs, 'ropes', 'wrestles', 'beats', 'parches', 'stanches', 'starches'.

ropes (line 5): used for the alliteration, but suggests swirling—often used by Hopkins in his Journal when talking of cloudscapes.

yestertempest (line 6): a typical economy of words.

in pool and rut peel, etc. (lines 6–7): Bridges suggested that rut-peel is a compound word and the fourth edition inscapes it into one word. The MS. is uncertain. W. H. Gardner suggests peel = 'cakes of mud from wheels'. Following Bridges's suggestion, the whole clause might be paraphrased as follows: 'In pool and rut the wind parches (dries) the squandering (viscous) mud, first to a kind of dough, then to stiff crust and finally to dust'.

stanches, starches, etc. (lines 7–9): i.e. dries-up, then stiffens and powders all the myriads of marks and footprints [that] treadmire toil has footfretted (stamped) on the mud. Cf. 'God's Grandeur' (lines 5–6).

nature's bonfire (line 9): all the above has been an illustration of the endless energy of creation and destruction that Heraclitus called the 'ever-living Fire', that is the world of Nature.

But quench (line 10): the syntax is obscure but the meaning is clear enough. In this Heraclitean meditation upon life it seems that the lives of all men are caught up in this eternal flux, and that they must suffer obliteration like everything else. 'Man is kindled, and put out like a light in the night', wrote Heraclitus.

clearest-selvèd spark (line 10): most distinctive creature (because possessed of reason and self-consciousness). See note p. 65) on 'The Sea and the Skylark'—'Life's pride and cared-for crown' (line 11).

firedint (line 11): probably each man's forged feature' (see Purcell sonnet, p. 90), his bodily aspect. Hopkins is thinking in Heraclitean terms of man's body as a mark on, or embodiment of, the Fire which constitutes all things. 'Dint' = blow, stamp, mark.

mark on mind (line 11): Hopkins wrote to Bridges that a 'great deal of early Greek philosophical thought' had been 'distilled' into this sonnet (*B*, 291). 'His mark on mind', therefore, refers to the 'mark' of each man's individual mind on the universal Reason which Heraclitus believed to be present in the world, itself a manifestation of the central Fire. It is concluded that man's individual mind is just as subject to total extinction as his body. All things come to be, and are then annihilated in the eternal flux.

Hopkins himself believed man's mind, as distinct from his body, to be the most distinctive and highly wrought aspect of creation. 'Nothing else in nature comes near this unspeakable stress of pitch, distinctiveness and selving, this self being of my own. Nothing explains or resembles it' (Comment on Spiritual Exercises of St Ignatius Loyola; S, 123).

He also believed in 'universal mind' of which the individual mind is a distinct manifestation.

The universal mind is outside of my inmost self and not within it: nor does it share my state, my moral standing, or my fate. And for all that this universal being may be at work in mine, it leaves me finite: I am self-existent none the more for any part the self-existent plays in me.
(ibid., 126)

The syntax of line 11 reads 'how fast man's body is gone, and how fast too his mind also is gone'.

Both (line 12): i.e. body and mind.

disseveral (line 14): compound word: distinct/severed/among several.

stark (line 15): clear and indelible. The syntax of these lines is as follows: 'Death blots out even man with all his uniqueness; nor is there any memory or trace of him which is not finally obliterated by time.'

vastness (line 16): Hopkins talked elsewhere (S, 122) of the 'vastness of the world' meaning the enormous abundance and variety of creation, out of which human nature has been 'condensed'.

Enough (line 16): his mood changes, as he reacts from the sombre thoughts to which he has been led by his Heraclitean meditation, to a realization of his Christian faith in personal immortality.

my foundering deck (line 18): shipwreck, to Hopkins, was always a potent image of personal despair. See note on 'The Wreck of the Deutschland', st. 1, p. 36.

residuary (line 20): legal term qualifying 'worm' which disposes of that which is left (i.e. 'flesh—mortal trash') when the soul has gone to its immortality. Here, as in 'The Sea and the Skylark' Hopkins tends to the Greek doctrine of the immortality of the soul, and consequent contempt for the body. Resurrection of the Body as well as soul is the full Christian doctrine.

world's wildfire (line 20): i.e. as portrayed in first 9 lines. The poet is calling on the 'wildfire' to do what it will—it cannot destroy man.

at a trumpet crash (line 21): this is an echo of the famous passage 1 Cor., xv, 51 et seq.:

We shall not sleep, but we shall all be changed, in a moment in the twinkling of an eye at the last trump: for the trumpet shall sound, and the dead shall be raised incorruptible, and we shall be changed. For this corruptible must put on incorruption and this mortal must put on immortality.

what Christ is (line 22): i.e. immortal and eternal.

he was what I am (line 22): again St Paul, 2 Cor., v, 21. God made Christ who knew no sin 'to be sin for us'. Since He has taken our sin upon Himself, we can receive His immortality.

Jack (line 23): poor contemptible creature.

potsherd (line 23): piece of broken pottery.

patch (line 23): fool.

diamond (line 23): symbol of purity, agelessness and value—also of pledge and promise.

Metre: Hopkins called this a sonnet with 2 codas, i.e. extra 'bars' of 2, 3 or 4 lines each at the end. Actually, as Bridges pointed out it has 3 codas. First 14 lines are classical sonnet rhyme scheme. Fifteenth line 'stark' echoes fourteenth and introduces 3 rhymed triplets, each of 2 long and 1 short line.

Rhythm is sprung rhythm with many 'outriding feet' (see Introduction, p. 16). All the longer lines have 6 stresses.

St Alphonsus Rodriguez
(Dublin, 1888)

On 3 October 1888, Hopkins wrote to Bridges:
I ask your opinion of a sonnet written to order on the occasion of the first feast since his canonization proper of St Alphonsus Rodriguez, a laybrother of our Order, who for 40 years acted as hall-porter to the College of Palma in Majorca: he was, it is believed, much favoured by God with heavenly lights and much persecuted by evil spirits. The sonnet (I say it snorting) aims at being intelligible.
(*B*, 292–3)
To this letter Hopkins appended the first version of the sonnet, rather different from the final form shown here.

Laybrother: one who joins a religious order and comes under the vows of poverty, chastity and obedience, without aspiring to the priesthood.
Honour is flashed off, etc. (line 1): the thought is that honour is given to men for outward conquests alone. Hopkins is going to prove that God can also crown a career of inner and silent conquest.
tongue (line 3): verb, meaning 'give utterance to'. The 'strokes (marks of battle) should be memorials of honour on the body and shield of the hero who sustains them.
forge (line 4): stamp a visible memorial of.
they do (line 5): i.e. forge, etc., referring to Christ's five wounds by which He is known to the world. See 'The Wreck of the Deutschland', st. 22 and note (p. 45).
But be the war, etc. (line 6): i.e. if the war is, etc.
hurtle (line 8): noise. Cf. 'Before me the hurtle of hell' ('The Wreck of the Deutschland', st. 3).
Yet God that hews (line 9): In original version 'Yet God the mountain-mason, continent-quarrier, earthwright'. Bridges (although agnostic) called this imagery 'cheeky', causing Hopkins to alter it to its present form.
trickling increment (line 10): imperceptible growth, a deliberate contrast to the mighty acts of creation ('hews') by which continents are formed. Bridges, somewhat oddly, objected to the literal accuracy of the contrast— continents also are made by 'trickling increment', he said—but Hopkins had his way.
conquest (line 12): the lifelong inner battle with 'evil spirits' which was the lot of St Alphonsus and, of course, of Hopkins himself whose inner struggles were equally terrible. Whether he consciously meant it or not, this

sonnet is as much an image of his own 'war within' as of that of St Alphonsus.

without event (line 13): i.e. without outward happening. The obscurity and hard grind which is the price to be paid in the religious life was a frequent thought with Hopkins. See the 'sheer plod' in 'The Windhover', also 'The Wreck of the Deutschland', st. 27.

Metre: Sonnet form in standard (not sprung) rhythm. There are roughly 10 syllables per line, some having heavy stresses, e.g. 'gashed', 'galled', 'earth', 'out'. There are some elisions (syllables run almost together), e.g.

'*Unseen, the heroic*' l. 7, '*by of world*' l. 13.

'Thou art indeed just, Lord, if I contend'
(17 March 1889)

In private notes to a retreat, 1 January 1888, Hopkins had written:
I was continuing this train of thought this evening when I began to enter on that course of loathing and hopelessness which I have so often felt before, which made me fear madness and led me to give up the practice of meditation except, as now, in retreat and here it is again. I could therefore do no more than repeat 'Justus es, Domine, et rectum judicium tuum'[1] *and the like ... What is my wretched life? Five wasted years almost have passed in Ireland. I am ashamed of the little I have done, of my waste of time, although my helplessness and weakness is such that I could scarcely do otherwise ... All my undertakings miscarry: I am like a straining eunuch. I wish then for death; yet if I died now I should die imperfect, no master of myself, and that is the worst failure of all. O my God, look down on me.*
(*S*, 262)
The Latin epigraph—of which the first 3 lines of the poem are a rendering —is a heartcry of the prophet Jeremiah. The *RSV*—the original version of which was published in England 1881–5—reads:
Righteous art thou O Lord when I complain to thee;
yet I would plead my case before thee.
Why does the way of the wicked prosper?
Why do all who are treacherous thrive?
(Jer., xii, 1; cf. Job, x, 2)
Defeat, thwart me (line 7): an Englishman in Ireland, unwillingly associated with the Home Rule cause which his Irish Jesuit colleagues espoused but which he believed to be unlawful, Hopkins wrote:
I do not feel then that outwardly I do much good, much that I care to do or can much wish to prosper; and this is a mournful life I lead.
(*S*, 262)
fretty chervil (line 11): a kind of wild parsley, with 'fretty' (delicately fringed) leaves.
birds build—but not I build (line 12): a Miltonic thought and cadence. Cf. the rhythm of:
>   *Thus with the year*
> *Seasons return, but not to me returns*
> *Day, or the sweet approach of even or morn.*
(*Paradise Lost*, Bk. III, 40–2)

[1] *Thou art just, O Lord, and thy judgment is right.*

Time's eunuch (line 13): 'all impulse fails me: I can give myself no sufficient reason for going on. Nothing comes: I am a eunuch—but it is for the kingdom of heaven's sake' (Letter to Bridges, 12 January 1888).
wakes (line 13): i.e. lives.
send my roots rain (line 14): 'There is a point with me in matters of any size when I must absolutely have encouragement as much as crops rain' (*B*, 218–19).

Metre: A sonnet in standard rhythm. 'Observe, it must be read *adagio molto* and with great stress' (*B*, 303).

'The shepherd's brow, fronting forked lightning, owns'
(April 1889)

This sonnet is dated April 1889 and can be grouped with some of the poems of desolation. It is a remarkable outburst of wry cynicism now deservedly placed, in the fourth edition, in the canon of main poems. Bridges included it in the Hopkins fragments because he felt that the poem 'must have been thrown off one day in a cynical mood, which he would not have wished permanently to intrude among his last serious poems' (Notes to first edition). Since, however, Hopkins drafted it out at least five times, it is plain that Bridges, although acting with prudence at a time when negative feelings were not regarded as fit material for public poetic expression, might have reconsidered his decision in this franker day and age.

The poem is indeed a frank expression of disgust at human nature and of a sense of the futility of life. It is earthy and almost Jacobean in intensity and reminds one of Webster, the only difference being that in Hopkins's case it is a single and isolated outburst, against his normal and carefully maintained idealism. Today we would recognize such outbursts as legitimate safety valves for pent-up emotion, though a high-minded Victorian would hardly have approved of it. Hopkins, although himself a high-minded Victorian in many ways, was driven to a greater degree of emotional honesty than his age conventionally permitted.

The argument is roughly as follows: There is majesty, glory and horror in the world of nature and in the world of the supernatural. But what is there, either of glory or tragedy, in human nature? Nothing. Man, whatever fame he may achieve, is an insignificant and ephemeral little animal. With this sobering thought I [the poet] cool my idealistic ardours.

fronting (line 1): confronting, facing.
owns (line 1): acknowledges.
Angels fall . . . (lines 3–4) an idea suggested by the forked lightning, the reference being to the aboriginal cataclysm in the world of spirit mentioned in St Luke's Gospel—'I beheld Satan as lightning fall from heaven' (Luke, x, 18).
majestical, and giant groans (line 4): the words remind one of Milton's thunderous lines on Satan's fall:

>   *Him the Almighty Power*
> *Hurled headlong flaming from the ethereal sky*
> *With hideous ruin and combustion down*
> *To bottomless perdition, there to dwell*

In adamantine chains and penal fire,
Who durst defy the Omnipotent to arms.
(*Paradise Lost*, I, 44–9)

scaffold of score brittle bones (line 5): the idea of the body being a kind of death-house was very present to Hopkins—see 'The Caged Skylark' or 'I wake and feel the fell of dark, not day'. He often harks back, quite naturally to Renaissance imagery, to express it. That 'rich and nervous' Renaissance poet Andrew Marvell, wrote of a soul imprisoned:

With bolts of Bones, that fettered stands
In Feet; and manacled in Hands.
('Dialogue between the Soul and the Body')

groundlong (line 6): presumably means prone and helpless.

Memento mori (line 7): means literally 'remember you must die', but, used as a noun, means 'reminder of death'. The frailty of the flesh and the omnipresence of death in it was vividly expressed by Webster in an image that may have been in Hopkins's mind:

What's this flesh? a little crudded milk, fantastical puff-paste. Our bodies are weaker than those paper-prisons boys used to keep flies in; more contemptible, since ours is to preserve earthworms.
(*The Duchess of Malfi*, IV, ii, 121)

That Hopkins was acquainted with this passage is possibly confirmed by its being the lines immediately preceding those which refer to the 'turf of grass' which supplied an image for 'The Caged Skylark' (q.v.).

What bass . . . tones? (line 8): the sense of the question is: 'What is it in human life that can lend a note of dignity or tragedy?' The viol is a deep-noted bass violin, predecessor of the violoncello. The notes to the fourth edition of Hopkins's poems point to some lines in Isaiah which associate viols and cold mortality:

Thy pomp is brought down to the grave, and the noise of thy viols: the worm is spread under thee, and the worms cover thee.
(Isaiah, xiv, 11)

He! (line 9): i.e. man.

voids (line 9): excretes. A gloomy (to Hopkins) and perennial reminder of our basic animality.

blazoned in however bold the name (line 10): i.e. whatever fame he may achieve.

Man Jack the man is (line 11): 'Jack' is an expression used by Hopkins to denote ordinary and even contemptible aspects of himself and other men. See similar usages and notes on them in 'That Nature is a Heraclitean Fire', and in 'My own heart let me more have pity on'.

And I that die these deaths (line 12): he is alluding to his own, often futile, idealistic strivings, and to his frequent, and equally futile, anguish at the delinquency of men. See, for instance, 'Thou art indeed just, Lord, if I contend', the sonnet immediately preceding this one.

That . . . (line 13): on the brink of launching into a tirade, he halts in his tracks, as if to say 'Why bother?'

in smooth spoons . . . *mirrored* (line 13): he has a sudden vision of life as one might see it reflected in the concave/convex of a spoon, distorted, bulbous and ridiculous. One cannot help being reminded of T. S. Eliot's later allusion to the futility of life, spoken through the mouth of J. Alfred Prufrock: 'I have measured out my life with coffee spoons.' It is the same image, though used somewhat differently.

tame/My tempests there (lines 13–14): this thought of the farcical futility of life helps to pour cold water on his heated and fussy strivings.

Metre: A sonnet constructed after the Petrarchan' type—i.e. an octet (or rather two quartets) and a sestet. As usual Hopkins uses a tight, and technically more difficult, economy of rhyme in the octet. Other technical features are the feminine (two-syllable) rhymes, used here to impart an ironic echo to his meditations. Apart from line 3, which is definitely 'sprung', having no less than 15 syllables, the sonnet is in standard metre, heavily counterpointed.

To R.B.
(22 April 1888)

A sonnet written a year before his death and dedicated to Robert Bridges, his lifelong friend, confidant, fellow-poet and the one who, with patience and perseverance, was eventually to bring Hopkins's poetry before a world slow to understand it.

The poem is about the impoverishment of his creative gift, 'the roll, the rise, the carol, the creation'. He wrote to Dixon in the same year: 'My muse has long put down her carriage and now for years "takes in washing." The laundry is driving a great trade now.' (*D*, 157).

After the prolonged bout of mental torment suffered in 1884–5 his health had recovered a little, perhaps because he partly took his own advice to be to his 'sad self hereafter kind'. Nevertheless, he was often weak and dejected, 'in a distress of mind difficult both to understand and to explain', he wrote to Bridges (*B*, 282). The burden of his duties, especially with regard to the great quantities of examination papers he had to mark, preyed on his mind in this state of weakness, and left him without spirit for all his private interests. 'I see no ground for thinking I shall ever get over it', he wrote to Baillie, 'or ever succeed in doing anything that is not forced on me to do of any consequence' (*FL*, 256).

Perhaps too, as Father Devlin suggests, his powers were undergoing a period of change, 'a transition which seems common to all great English poets in middle age, from the delight of self-expression to a graver and more detached labour of creation' (*S*, 219–20). In his case the dryness of his sensibility was accompanied by an inability to pray and a haunting sense of failure in all things. It was from this 'winter world' that he wrote this sonnet.

The fine delight that fathers thought (line 1): i.e. the joyful surge of spirit that produces creative thought. In an early letter (1864) to Baillie, Hopkins wrote of 'poetry proper, the language of inspiration':
The word inspiration need cause no difficulty. I mean by it a mood of great, abnormal in fact, mental acuteness, either energetic or receptive ... The mood arises from various causes, physical generally, as good health or state of the air or, prosaic as it is, length of time after a meal. But I need not go into this; all that it is needful to mark is, that the poetry of inspiration can only be written in this mood of mind, even if it only lasts a minute.
(*FL*, 216)
Nine months she then, nay years (line 5): a beautiful line achieved by alliter-

ating the consonants and varying the vowel sounds within the alliterative pattern. This long period of gestation of a poem was in fact the case with Hopkins:

'We greatly differ in feeling about copying one's verses out,' he wrote to Bridges, 'I find it repulsive, and let them lie months and years in rough copy untransferred to my book' (*B*, 304).

combs (line 6): the image is still that of a mother, in this case lovingly combing and tending her child's hair.

The widow of an insight lost (line 7): the spark of inspiration which conceived the poem may have gone, but the mind (the 'widow') now knows her 'aim', to give it body and bring it forth to the world.

Sweet fire the sire of muse (line 9): same as 'The fine delight that fathers thought'.

My winter world (line 13): Hopkins's accounts of his inner state during these years, though often humorous, always reveal the underlying pain. This, for instance, to Bridges in 1887:

Tomorrow morning I shall have been three years in Ireland, three hard wearying wasting wasted years. (I met the blooming Miss Tynan again this afternoon. She told me that when she first saw me she took me for 20 and some friend of hers for 15; but it won't do: they should see my heart and vitals, all shaggy with the whitest hair.) In those I have done God's will (in the main) and many many examination papers.

(*B*, 250–1)

that bliss (line 13): i.e. 'the one rapture of an inspiration'.

Now, yields you, with some sighs, our explanation (line 14): a flat nerveless finish, deliberately contrived to evoke the barrenness of which the poet has been complaining. It should be added, however, that 'the roll, the rise, the carol, the creation', have been present, especially in the octet, even as Hopkins mourned their loss.

Metre: Standard sonnet rhythm—iambic pentameter—with some 'hurried feet', e.g.

1.4. *Leaves yet the mind a mother of immortal song.*

1.7. *The widow of an insight lost she lives, with aim.*

Short Glossary

Short Glossary

A list of some of Hopkins's distinctive usages—dialect forms, archaisms and obsolete words, coinages, and ordinary words used in an unusual way.

arch-especial, 89

baldbright, 79
barrowy, 170
beadbonny, 118
beetling, 79
began (n.), 156
betweenpie, 164
bole, 79
  beechbole, 170
brandle, 101
breathed, 169
brinded, 70
broth, 169
buck, 43
burl, 43

chevy (v.), 172
cobbled, 43
cogged, 128
combes, 61
coop, 117
cringe, 42
crossbridle (v.), 170
curded, 170

dapple, 70, 84, 136
degged, 118
delves (n.), 57
dint, 173
disremembering, 136
disseveral, 174

easter, (v.) 50

fagged, 128
fashed, 128
feature, 90
fell (n.), 158
fetch (n.), 44
fettle (v.), 112
firefeaturing, 136
fleece, 118, 126
flitches, 118
flixed, 131
flue, 169
forgèd, 90
fretty, 178
furled, 49, 79

hallows (n.), 58
hawling, 44
heavengravel, 80
housel, 99
hurtle, 176

Jack, 175, 181
  Jackself, 164
justices (v.), 120

keeping (n.), 87

leafmeal, 115
louched, 122
lovescape, 45

mammock (v.), 165

Index

Index